Do You Really Know Who You Are?

Do you know how you look to others? Find out all about yourself—even the things you dislike. Your chance for happiness and fulfillment is so easy, if you reach for it.

Be the Person You Were Meant to Be offers a dramatically effective new way of changing your life style by looking at yourself and becoming a whole new you.

Read it—and start it all happening today.

ABOUT THE AUTHOR: *Dr. Jerry Greenwald* is one of America's most successful therapists and a frequent contributor to leading professional journals.

Be the Person You Were Meant to Be

(ANTIDOTES TO TOXIC LIVING)

Dr. Jerry Greenwald

FOR PATTI, LYNDA AND MICHAEL

Published by
DELL PUBLISHING CO., INC.
1 Dag Hammarskjold Plaza
New York, New York 10017

Printed in the United States of America
October 1974
10 9 8 7 6

WFH

Acknowledgments

I wish to express my appreciation to Frederick Perls, M.D., Ph.D., and James Simkin, Ph.D., from whom I have assimilated the philosophy of Gestalt Therapy and made it part of myself and my existence.

I want to thank Gloria Johnson for her continuous encouragement and insights which contributed greatly to this book. I also want to thank Joan Rydbeck for her invaluable assistance in the preparation of the manuscript.

Contents

Preface

The philosophy of Gestalt holds that a person need not undo, work through, or otherwise eliminate the toxic effects of past experiences by delving into them. On the contrary, the deliberate attempt to probe into the past for this purpose simply perpetuates the destructive power of these obsolete experiences which belong to the reality of an earlier era of the person's life. They serve largely to distort the reality of his present functioning, his concept of his self, and his ways of relating to the world.

There is a beautiful simplicity and optimism about the philosophy of Gestalt. Granted that past relationships and experiences have shaped an individual's attitudes and ways of reacting in the present, the letting go of those attitudes and behavior patterns which are toxic begins the moment one focuses his attention on the present. The healthy person is in contact with his experiencing (thinking, feeling, acting) self in the present. His functioning is expressed in appropriate reactions and behavior based on his experiencing of the now. When he has "come to his senses," he cannot at the same time poison himself with his fears, anxieties, phobias, and catastrophic expectations based on past traumatic experiences.

In Gestalt, reality exists only in the present. A person's memory of the past (despite his sincere denials of this fact) is a collection of obsolete distortions and misperceptions. His future is an assortment of anticipations and anxieties (catastrophic expectations) of which the overwhelming proportion never materialize at all and of which those that do, rarely fit the agonizing preparations to which he may have devoted enormous energy for counteracting them.*

In his principal book, *Gestalt Therapy*,† Frederick S. Perls states that the philosophy of Gestalt therapy is a statement of what is natural about man and life. This approach makes no assumptions and postulates no hypothetical explanations about what a human being is like.

This book utilizes the philosophy of Gestalt therapy to explore natural and unnatural behavior. The intent is to minimize the reader's unnatural (toxic) behavior in relating to himself and others and to emphasize the discovery of natural (nourishing) attitudes and behavior patterns.

The goal of Gestalt therapy is to melt the toxic power of the past by learning to focus on the present. When a person lives wholly in the now, the past with

* The "unchanging reality" of the past and present is taken for granted. For example, a person learns to read during childhood, and his knowledge of reading remains valid. A father aware that his death is unpredictable takes out a life-insurance policy for his family.
† Frederick S. Perls, M.D., Ph.D.; Ralf F. Helfferlind, Ph.D.; and Paul Goodman, Ph.D., Julian Press, Inc., 1958.

all its destructive effects recedes into the background of his behavior and loses its power.

Discovering how to live a more nourishing, creative, and fulfilling life has endless potentials. When a person is interested, he begins the process of becoming aware of himself and how he functions in the here and now. It is irrelevant whether he is eight or eighty. The common attitude of middle-aged and older people that "it's too late for me to change" is simply an example of an obsolete, toxic attitude.

Much of this book focuses on the many ingenious ways in which people avoid the reality of their present existence. Each person's awareness of how he does this is the gateway to the discovery of antidotes for his own self-poisoning processes and those he allows to be inflicted upon him by others. What can be even more exhilarating is the discovery that each time he frees himself from any toxic process he liberates an enormous amount of trapped energy which he can now utilize for more creative and gratifying purposes.

A further aim of this book is to help the reader become more aware of how he nourishes and poisons himself and his relationships. Awareness is an endlessly available opportunity offering the possibilities of new discoveries of who one is—and who one isn't. This limitless potential to experience the joy and excitement of learning about oneself and one's world can make life a meaningful adventure for anyone.

It takes effort for a person to be willing to risk experimenting with new attitudes and behavior as he undertakes to discover a more nourishing life style. It has long been recognized that without some kind of frustration (tension or deprivation) a person will not be motivated to do anything. In this sense, the pain of frustration is necessary for change. Unfortunately, most of the emotional pain people experience is largely unnecessary. People are unwilling to "listen" to their pain and therefore allow it to persist. Similarly, there are countless ways people anesthetize their pain and thereby create a toxic stalemate which may go on indefinitely. Hopefully, this book will enable the person to confront himself with his own pattern of avoidance and his own ways of blocking his awareness so that he can begin more effectively to respond to them and seek his antidotes.

Toxic influences of many kinds are always present. Any individual can enhance his awareness and develop more effective antidotes against the toxic influences in his personal life. His natural self relentlessly pushes toward health and growth. These potentials for self-fulfillment are never lost or destroyed. However, in countless ways he buries them, tears himself apart with inner conflicts, struggles against fantasized enemies, and projects his power and his problems onto other people. These are the toxic behavior patterns which actively hamper our natural growth. They can be minimized, however, through the discovery and use of effective antidotes. This in turn frees the person's capacity to experience the joy and excitement of living his life fully and discovering more of his untapped resources and potentials.

Nourishing or toxic behavior is valid only when it is based on the individual's own understanding of how he can control his own well-being. Even when a person is in a grave crisis of despair or anxiety and feels totally helpless, he is still the one who is most capable of discovering a solution to his problems. This book does not attempt to offer answers to specific dilemmas;

it seeks to help every individual to utilize his own latent potentials for standing on his own two feet and discovering for himself what he needs to live a nourishing life.

CHAPTER ONE

Nourishing and Toxic Living

How do we go about living a nourishing life? How do we discover what it is that we do that is nourishing or toxic to our well-being and that of others? This quest is not nearly as complicated as most people imagine. Becoming more aware of one's behavior *is* the beginning of change. This process begins with awareness of our attitudes and ways of relating to ourselves. The basic question is: How do I go about nourishing and poisoning myself?

In the following questions, the reader can check for himself whether his existing behavior patterns are largely nourishing or toxic.

1. **Nourishing:** Do I take the initiative in doing the best I can to get what I need?

    or

    Toxic: Do I wait and hope that somehow what I need will be brought to me by someone else?

2. **Nourishing:** Do I decide what's most important for me?

    or

Toxic: Do I allow others to make decisions for me?

3. **Nourishing:** Do I give up my attempts to control the world and accept life as it is?

or

Toxic: Do I live my life dominated by fears of catastrophe for which I continuously attempt to prepare?

4. **Nourishing:** Am I willing to take reasonable risks and experiment with new behavior that might be more satisfying?

or

Toxic: Do I cling to obsolete behavior patterns which mainly offer the security of being familiar?

5. **Nourishing:** Do I focus on what I am doing in the here and now?

or

Toxic: Do I usually wander into fantasies of the future or mistakes about the past?

6. **Nourishing:** Do I pay attention to one experience at a time?

or

Toxic: Do I try to do two things at once and thereby split my attention into pieces?

7. **Nourishing:** Do I take for myself the central role of determining my life style?

or

Toxic: Do I give over this function to others?

8. **Nourishing:** Do I take responsibility for satisfying my own needs?

or

Toxic: Do I try to manipulate other people into doing it for me?

9. **Nourishing:** Do I function as best I can in the here and now of my life?

   or

   Toxic: Do I cling to the misfortunes and tragedies of my past (real or imagined) and use these as excuses to avoid taking responsibility for myself in the present?

10. **Nourishing:** Do I live my personal life as I see fit and take my chances that some people will reject me?

    or

    Toxic: Do I go through life explaining myself and needing everyone's approval?

11. **Nourishing:** Do I see life as exciting and stimulating?

    or

    Toxic: Do I experience myself struggling to stay alive in a jungle of hostile forces?

12. **Nourishing:** Do I see myself as continuing to grow to the last day of my life?

    or

    Toxic: Do I create an artificial cutoff (*e.g.*, "After thirty it's all downhill") and live as if my opportunities for new discoveries and new-found joys were over?

13. **Nourishing:** Do I accept my need for other people as part of my life style?

    or

    Toxic: Do I "let it all hang out" and if others don't like it, "Who needs them"?

14. **Nourishing:** Do I experience my conflicts and "problems" as essentially of my own making?

    or

Toxic: Do I project these onto other people and blame them for my troubles?

15. **Nourishing:** Is my behavior primarily self-regulating and based on my discoveries of what fits me?

or

Toxic: Do I cling to attitudes instilled in me in my childhood which I am afraid to reject?

16. **Nourishing:** Do I accept myself as I am and decide how I wish to change if at all?

or

Toxic: Do I believe that I *must* become a different person in order to live a nourishing, gratifying life?

17. **Nourishing:** Am I willing to take the risks of reaching out for what I want?

or

Toxic: Am I so fearful of rejection that I would rather starve myself emotionally than risk being turned down?

18. **Nourishing:** Do I experience my feelings and emotions as valuable parts of myself?

or

Toxic: Do I see them as weaknesses to be controlled and suppressed?

19. **Nourishing:** Am I aware of the changing reality of myself and the world around me?

or

Toxic: Do I rigidly insist on my established attitudes and values as fixed and unchangeable?

20. **Nourishing:** Do I accept my mistakes as an inevitable part of learning?

or

Toxic: When I do something that displeases me do I attack myself with ridicule, disgust or self-punishment?

21. **Nourishing:** Do I focus on the gratifications and meaningfulness of day-to-day experiences as the essence of living a nourishing life?

or

Toxic: Do I toil without satisfaction, working toward the day when, hopefully, I will "be happy"?

22. **Nourishing:** Do I center my attention on appreciating what I enjoy in my experiencing of myself and my world?

or

Toxic: Do I focus on what's lacking or what I find frustrating?

23. **Nourishing:** Do I accept myself as I am and continue my growth primarily as something I want for myself?

or

Toxic: Do I stand condemned in my own eyes as inadequate and seek to "prove" myself by accomplishments or success?

24. **Nourishing:** Do I experience my selfishness as an expression of the law of self-preservation?

or

Toxic: Do I believe that "selfishness" is a dirty word?

25. **Nourishing:** Do I accept pain as a normal aspect of living and an inevitable aspect of my growth?

or

Toxic: Do I experience pain (anxiety, tension, fearfulness) as something "evil"?

26. **Nourishing.** Am I aware that pain is often a valuable message directing my attention toward some frustrated need which I am neglecting?

or

Toxic: Do I consider pain as something to be immediately minimized or eliminated in any way possible?

27. **Nourishing:** Is my behavior a reaction to my experiencing of present reality?

or

Toxic: Do I project my past experiences onto the present?

Natural functioning is determined by our capabilities and potentials. Toxic influences are those which violate this natural functioning. It is a natural function, based on physiological structure, for the infant to defecate on biological demand. His structure is such that his body spontaneously forces out waste material. He lacks the muscular ability to constrain his need to defecate. Thus, toilet training in early infancy is a toxic intrusion. It is an attempt to modify the infant's functioning by placing an unnatural and unrealistic demand on the existing structure. In an effort to respond to this kind of toxic demand, the infant's body begins to tighten and lose its gracefulness. He becomes awkward and inhibited.

It is unreasonable to suggest that a person can be spontaneous at all times, even in early childhood, and still function in a group. Social living inevitably demands numerous restraints on the spontaneity of each person. Since our society provides us with many satisfactions and gratifications (nourishment), some pressure is a necessary part of the reality of group living. Pressure becomes toxic, however, when it is unrealistic or excessive in the limitations it places on our spontaneity. The toxic intrusion in this example could be lessened by a delay in toilet training until the infant's structure (sphincter muscles) has developed sufficiently to be capable of the task demanded and until he can comprehend what he is being asked to inhibit (regulate).

Psychological theories about human behavior, however valid, are abstractions. They consist largely of masses of information, data, or speculations that have been formulated into a composite picture of man. When a person attempts to live his life on the basis of such theories, he traps himself by subjugating his aliveness to the abstractions of how he "should" be. "Unless you work through the neurotic fixations of your repressed childhood experiences, you cannot possibly be happy." Or, "Until you have resolved your Oedipal complex, your interpersonal relationships will remain on an infantile level." Or, "If you will meditate for two hours a day and give up eating meat, you will find greater peace and contentment." Many people "shop" for psychological theories, or seek guidance of others instead of attempting to seek an identity of their own.

To use an analogy, when we need clothes we go to a favorite store and choose what we like best—but no matter how discriminating we may be, we end up wearing someone else's creation. Other factors may further preclude our personal preference. Rather than choose what we really like best, we may yield to the pressure of current fashions, the attitude of the salesman, the opinion of a friend, and various other outside influences. Through our mistakes we can learn to be increasingly discriminating about whom we listen to. We may even discover a style that particularly suits us. Nevertheless, we have not learned to create our own designs and weave our own cloth so that what we wear is truly our own creation. While this is not so important in selecting one's wardrobe, it is essential in selecting experiences that are self-nourishing. As adults, it is primarily our responsibility to utilize our potential to weave the cloth and fashion the style of our own identity.

We move into adulthood with a large quantity of accumulated experience, data, and attitudes that have been offered or forced on us throughout our childhood. For the most part, we grow up with overwhelming restrictions on how our identity—our individual uniqueness—is allowed to evolve and express itself. Almost without exception, the child is dominated by the attitudes and values of others. In reality he is not free to be his own person. As the child matures, his power to discover and express his individuality increases, and with this power come more options to be the way *he* chooses to be. Past experiences are, of course, a major factor in determining our attitudes and behavior in adulthood. However, it is absurd to assume that we are stuck with the ways of being we learned during childhood and adolescence. Such a notion violates the obvious fact that life itself is a process of change. When we become interested in committing ourselves to the lifelong adventure of discovering our own selves, we enthusiastically grasp the full responsibility for discovering what we experience as meaningful and nourishing and minimizing what we find empty or toxic.

Two days after Sharon graduated from high school, she found a job as a waitress. The day she received her first pay check, she rented an apartment. Until then, she had never spent a single night away from her parents. Sharon had managed to survive a desperate childhood in which she was dominated by a tyrannical father who ruthlessly played on her need for approval and her deep feelings of inadequacy. She tried hard to please him, but he somehow managed to find fault with everything she did. He criticized her friends, teased her for her interest in boys, and constantly warned her that soon enough she would discover "what a lousy world it is out there."

As long as Sharon could remember, her mother had sought refuge in a mouselike retreat from a similar onslaught from her father. Powerless to take a stand against him and lacking any support from her mother, she too had "gone underground" when she entered high school.

When she left, she tried to explain to her father that she had to "find herself" and that living with him was too oppressive. He honestly didn't know what she was talking about; he threatened to disown her, and when that was ineffective, he accused her of being an ungrateful, unloving daughter and warned that she would soon come crawling back.

It is our responsibility to be aware when we are talking to a person who has no ears, and continue to hope that one day we will be heard.

Sharon finally "came to her senses" and realized that her father *could not* accept her as a separate individual, with her own needs.

Some superior governing power is inevitable when we live together, and this governing power unavoidably curtails our freedom of self-expression and our actions. We have little choice but to accept that we must to some degree submit to the power of group restrictions on our behavior. Similarly, when we are interested in relating to another person, it is just as inevitable that we must to some degree restrict our own spontaneity because of the needs and reactions of another person. Only the person who is out of contact with reality has the notion that he can be his total, spontaneous self and still maintain nourishing relationships with other individuals.

A person is authentic only when his behavior is self-regulating. We must all learn for ourselves what we do in response to our inner needs, our relationships with others, and our functioning within the structure of our society. In all these areas we are responsible for everything we do, in that we will experience the nourishing or toxic consequences of our own behavior. This *is* how we discover who we are. What we do and how we function *is* our self.

"N" PEOPLE AND "T" PEOPLE

As our proficiency in the art of emotional nourishment grows, each of us moves toward becoming a more nourishing person. This is an ongoing process throughout life. Developing and sustaining nourishing relationships begins with and depends on the nourishing qualities of each of us, and these qualities in turn

are reflected in our ability to select others who are
themselves more nourishing than toxic. The more
aware a person is of his own nourishing and toxic
qualities, the more effective his ability to seek out
others with whom he can establish meaningful, gratifying relationships.

For descriptive purposes, two groups of behavior
patterns are postulated. Those people who function
in a predominantly *nourishing* fashion are referred to
as N people. Those whose attitudes are predominantly
toxic will be referred to as T people. Each person is
both nourishing *and* toxic in varying degrees. Everyone's behavior fluctuates; the most nourishing person
behaves in a toxic manner at times, and the most
poisonous person is at times nourishing. These patterns
are dynamic and changing. In a sense, an individual is
always in the process of becoming more nourishing or
more toxic. We can discover our own N and T patterns
through greater awareness of how we experience our
self, how we experience our relationships with others,
and how others react to us.

Comparisons are drawn between N and T people
only for the purpose of increasing awareness of when
an experience is nourishing and when it is toxic. In
any relationship, each person is inevitably exposed to
both the nourishing and the toxic attitudes and behavior of the other. To develop a check list of nourishing
and toxic "qualities" or to diagnose or label a person
as one or the other is not only meaningless: it is itself
a toxic procedure. The essence of the art of emotional
nourishment is our awareness of what we are experiencing and our ability to accept nourishment and to
protect ourself against toxic behavior.

Nourishing and toxic patterns manifest themselves

in a remarkably consistent fashion as a person relates both to himself and to others. In this sense, the degree of emotional involvement with the various people with whom the person interacts is irrelevant. For example, a nourishing person is considerate of a salesclerk. How he relates to him will be consistent with his behavior toward his own spouse or child. His underlying N and T qualities will prevail. The woman who insults or degrades the clerk will also attack the egos of her own children. Perhaps more often than not, this basic consistency is concealed beneath the façades of phony behavior each person has learned. A very toxic person may give every appearance of being a loving, caring individual when the situation requires him to present this appearance.

Feelings of distrust and suspicion toward another are not necessarily "wrong," "bad," or otherwise unwarranted.

For N people, personal survival, growth, and the satisfaction of their basic needs are healthy manifestations. For them, selfishness (self-ness) is simply the recognition and acceptance of the reality that each person is the most important person in the world to himself. The N person is aware that he will be unable to give nourishment to others unless he sustains his own health. It is not surprising, then, that N people are more authentic and aware and have fulfilled more of their potentials. They value their integrity more and are better able to stand on their own two feet. Rather than lean on others, they assume responsibility for their own needs. They have greater willingness to state openly and directly what they want. In relationships, they are attracted to those who give freely. They obtain nourishment from others and give nourishment in the same process, much like a man who cares for a fruit tree: he enjoys its fruits and in turn prunes and fertilizes it, thereby enhancing its health and growth.

Toxic people manifest the opposite qualities. Typically, anyone the T person encounters is in some way left depleted by the encounter. Toxic people manifest excessive phoniness, manipulation, and deception. A T person's life pattern is one in which nourishment of his needs is detrimental to others, whom he uses for his own ends. In contrast to the self-reliant N person, the T person needs a continuous supply of people, since either he uses them up (*i.e.*, they get tired of being drained) or he gets restless and wants something more. His relationships in general tend to be unstable and superficial; the T person is therefore chronically dissatisfied.

Intimate relating means avoiding using our resources to manipulate the other person.

While N people are more available and responsive, their giving is not forced on others; it is offered. They do not try to persuade others into accepting their favors. Despite their genuine interest in giving, they do not intrude if the other expresses lack of interest. In turn, giving to N people is easy and gratifying. The N person is less demanding and more appreciative of what he receives. He handles his unfulfilled needs himself rather than burdening others with them.

A good self-nourisher is persistent in striving for what he wants. However, he does not put all his eggs in one basket. Toxic people often hunt compulsively for intense relationships and neglect all others, as if there were no point in appreciating anything less than the ideal. Nourishing people experience this compulsion to be intimate as toxic and intrusive and are apt to avoid this rigid way of relating.

The N person is better able to accept what he does not like in another, while appreciating what gratification he does find in the relationship. He does not, like the T person, simply cut people off because of their failings or withdraw permanently when they attempt to manipulate or use him in some way. Rather, he has a greater range of inner resources with which to cope with these occurrences in an ongoing relationship. He is more likely to be aware when he is being used, and he is better able to stop this from occurring or continuing. He can say "no" without annihilating the other person, and he can take his position in a disagreement without an excessive need to explain or justify himself. He does not need to win approval of his own actions from others. He can be rejecting toward another person at one time and still remain free to subsequently give to him.

The N person has greater awareness of his experiences and has greater ability to integrate these into his responsiveness. He uses his awareness to avoid manipulating others and to be more accepting of their limitations. He doesn't demand that the other do more than he is able or willing to do. If his eleven-year-old son has an I.Q. of 150 and a "C" average, he accepts his son's below-potential performance. He may feel concern and express his willingness to help in any way he can, but he doesn't try to force a change in behavior. The T parent, in contrast, uses a variety of manipulative techniques to "get" his son to improve.

N PARENT: I'd like to check with you about school. Are you having any problems or anything you want to talk about? *(Nourishing)*

SON: I guess you're unhappy about my low grades.

N PARENT: I would like to see you do better, but that's my attitude and I don't want to put it on you. *(Nourishing)* If you're satisfied with your grades, I'll accept that. *(Nourishing)*

SON: Well—the work is boring, and the teacher spends most of her time with the kids who are flunking. I . . . I've been reading other books and not turning in my assignments.

N.P.: How would you feel about my talking to the teacher about this? *(Nourishing)*

S.: No. I'm passing, and that's all I want. Maybe next year will be better.

N.P.: Okay. Let me know if there's anything I can do.

T PARENT: I'm disappointed in your report card. You should be doing a lot better. *(Toxic expectation)* You want to go to college, don't you? *(Toxic question demands a "yes" answer.)*

S (meekly with head down): Uh-huh.

T PARENT: Well, what's the trouble? You're lucky you've got the brains to do better. You should be ashamed bringing home such grades. *(Shame-inducing techniques are toxic.)*

S: Well, the class is boring, and the teacher—

T.P.: That's no excuse. Suppose I get bored working at the office and just goofed off and got
fired. How would you like me to tell you we
have to sell the house and move? *(Refuses to
listen to son; toxic analogy designed to induce
guilt.)*

S (upset): I'm sorry. I'll try to do better.

T.P.: I should hope so—it's for your own good, not
mine. Meanwhile, I want you to stop bringing
home all those other books from the library
until your grades improve. *(Toxic punishment).*

The N person is less prone to extreme actions of all
types. He is less violent and hostile—which does not,
however, imply that he lacks strength or determination. To the contrary, because he is more aware of
what values and goals are most central in his existence,
he is far more effective in striving for what he wants.
He has greater resourcefulness, flexibility, and adaptability because he doesn't poison himself with rigid
attitudes.

The T person, on the other hand, lacks flexibility
and elasticity. His relating to another may be stable
as long as he likes the give-and-take of the relationship. However, when he encounters conflict he is more
apt to end the relationship. The other person suddenly
becomes "no damn good." This dogmatic attitude is a
major factor in his excessive tendency to terminate
relationships and to find himself lonely and isolated.

The N person maintains flexibility in struggling for
what he believes in. He is able to fight, give ground,
counterattack, and, above all, continue the struggle
and see it through. The T person's convictions are

based more on fear and his subjugation to the dominance of others. He has a greater tendency to break and run under stress.

Toughness is a valuable human attribute. The N person can be very tough when the need arises, but he can do so without losing his warm, caring, and loving qualities.

Toxic people are not willfully destructive. To criticize a T person for his toxic behavior is itself a toxic attitude. One might as well condemn a rattlesnake as "evil" because its bite is poisonous. The T person is himself simply a product of too many toxic experiences and too few nourishing experiences, whether in his past or present life or both.

An aware N person will find his relationship with a T person to be largely a one-way street and will minimize such encounters. An unaware N person in a prolonged encounter with a T person will experience emotional drain and frustration more or less continually. Indeed, without awareness of how he is being poisoned by this kind of relationship, the N person may gradually become unhealthy and undernourished and eventually will himself manifest more of the behavior typical of T people.

Instead of being self-starters, T people tend to wait for cues or stimuli from others. Their overt behavior begins with a response to someone else. They tend to be "reactors to" rather than "initiators of" behavior. For example, the "clinging vine" wife becomes anxious and threatened when her husband wants to do something that happens to exclude her; the passive-dependent husband becomes angry, hurt, or resentful when his wife engages in some pursuit that excludes him. When left to his own devices, the T person often seems like a helpless child.

A T person seems incapable of making another person feel good. He refuses to give in a straightforward fashion with no strings attached. Any happiness a person experiences from a T person is apt to be short-lived or conditional. For example, having enjoyed a dinner, the appreciative guest-victim is told about the laborious effort involved in preparing the food, or receives hints of expected reciprocation. It is as if the T person were unwilling to please another without in some way contaminating the simple act of giving and bringing joy. He always wants the other person to feel indebted and grateful; often he insists on it. When his victim rebels, he is made to feel selfish and worthless. The "self-sacrificing" parent often controls adult children in this way. Again, the victim is emotionally drained to one degree or another.

The T person is also a poor receiver. When one gives to a T person, something about the manner in which the giving is received always contaminates the experience, not only for the giver but also for the recipient himself. For example, the adult who visits his elderly parent is thanked by the parent with some added comment to the effect that he doesn't come over as often as he should.

The ability to communicate is impaired in a T person. He doesn't listen. Someone seeking to express himself to a T person usually experiences frustration as he repeatedly tries to make his point. Married couples may repeat an almost identical argument for years and yet remain stalemated. Neither hears the other, and neither is genuinely interested in understanding the other's point of view. Conversation between T people consists of dialogue that does not reflect responsiveness to each other's statements. Rather, each has in mind what he will say before the other is finished. Experientially, their dialogue really consists of two unconnected monologues.

The excessive criticalness of the T person prevents him from accepting another person as he is and enjoying what he likes about him. Instead he focuses on the negative—on what he doesn't like. For example, when a T couple spends an evening with friends, their conversation afterward consists of critical, derogatory observations about the evening: what was wrong with the other guests, the host, the refreshments. The T person has a negative attitude toward himself and the world. He seems to be attracted to trouble and unhappiness. Often he appears suspiciously eager to hear about other people's problems. He rarely seems to enjoy himself. Instead, he concentrates on what has been bad or unsatisfactory about his experiences.

This attitude frequently accounts for the insatiability of the T person. His incessant demanding reflects his chronic dissatisfaction, for which he seeks to compensate by gorging himself. Since he is incapable of finding inner peace, his greed tends to be endless. It may take the form of a compulsive quest for money, material things, success, sex, food, or anything else that seems to promise some satisfaction. Frequently, the T person becomes even more desperate when he achieves "success," as he discovers that attaining his goal fails to bring the hoped-for happiness. He can then only redouble his efforts or fall into a state of depression.

Ted R. grew up on the East Side of New York City in abject poverty. His father supported the family of seven children by whatever means he could. He adamantly refused any charity or public assistance. Many times, they ate only one meal a day in their three-room, often unheated apartment.

Ted was determined to make a great deal of money. At fourteen he got his first job, shining shoes. At seventeen he went to work for a cabinetmaker, and four years later, when the owner died, he bought the business. He was not only bright, clever, and ambitious, but compulsively driven by his dread of ever being poor again. As his successes multiplied, he carefully invested his accumulated wealth in government bonds, blue-chip stocks, and paid-up life insurance.

He was forty-two when one day he was suddenly struck by the realization that even if he never earned another dollar, his income from his investments guaranteed him a life of wealth as long as the country itself existed. His narrow, compulsive life style had suddenly lost its purpose. He became panicked and desperate over the lack of meaning in his life. He began psychotherapy in a state of suicidal despair.

Living a nourishing life is an ongoing process of recognizing and responding to our changing needs and the changing reality of ourself and our world.

When he feels threatened, the T person tends to react impulsively and conclusively. His tolerance for threatening situations is limited, and he is less able to wait and delay his reactions. The N person, in contrast, has greater tolerance, and his reactions are more moderate and flexible.

The T person manifests an impressive variety of patterns with which he controls and manipulates others. These patterns are often subtle and deceptive. Sometimes he seems like an innocent, helpless, naïve individual who always needs to be rescued by someone else. The "hero" in such instances ultimately turns out to be the victim. The "hero" may go on hoping for years that if he does enough, the "helpless" person will finally become capable of standing on his own feet. The victim does not realize that his helpful attitude only deepens the trap as his emotional investment becomes greater and greater.

Some T people are control-mad. They seduce others into involvement with them, and once they win them over, they become openly domineering. By then, the victim is emotionally involved and may sacrifice his freedom and integrity in order to maintain the relationship—particularly if he is also T-oriented and willing to poison himself by continuing a toxic relationship.

Toxic people oppress those around them. For example, they talk incessantly and meaninglessly while their victims must listen politely or risk offending them. Their conversations reflect neither self-expression nor genuine desire for communication. There is frequently a close correlation between the meaninglessness of their conversation and the quantity of words they disgorge. In addition to their dull chatter, they may further oppress the atmosphere by their depression.

Toxic people fail to see others as individuals or to respect the integrity of others. In their sexual relationships they are selfish and inconsiderate. Rather than a mutually shared and enjoyed experience, sex to them is something one person does to another at the other's expense. T people see their sex partners as objects and often use sex, or withhold it, as a means of manipulation.

Other T people resent sharing, even when they have all they want, and they behave as if it pained them to see others have the same thing. They are so starved for nourishment, and so insecure about its continuing supply, that even when they experience some gratification, they need the added assurance of the deprivation of others. In their futile attempts to reassure themselves, they need to compare and come out on top.

Toxic people are less anxious when those around them are frustrated, unhappy, and generally miserable. They tend to surround themselves with such people, as if they feel comfort in a morbid human environment. On the other hand, they are often severely disturbed by happy, self-nourishing people. Either they try to pull others down into a state of misery similar to their own or they withdraw.

Nourishing people focus on what they find enjoyable, what they appreciate, what they find gratifying. The characteristic "hole-in-the-doughnut" attitude of T people contaminates the potential nourishment they might otherwise obtain. They obstruct their self-nourishing capabilities with their own psychological excrement. It is the T person, for example, who spots every candy wrapper and beer can in the park or forest and becomes obsessed with this aspect of his experience. To be sure, such debris is an unfortunate blemish, but the T person cheats himself of the nourishment of the beauty that is also present. It is ironic that T people, who are essentially emotionally deprived, are the very ones who are most apt to cheat themselves of the potential emotional enrichment of their own experiences.

Typically, T people lack autonomy and self-initiating abilities. They are phobic about using these resources for their own gratification, and therefore they are poor self-nourishers. Sometimes their helpless attitude is so extreme it appears they might starve if left to their own devices. They are usually phobic about loneliness and may spend their whole lives fearing abandonment. Their constant dependency on others for nourishment becomes self-defeating. They "suck" nourishment out of others, thereby destroying the desire of their overtaxed friends to continue the one-sided relationship. The T person's other-oriented focus further complicates his nourishment problem by lessening his chances of discovering his own potentials for self-nourishment. (Why do it yourself if you can manipulate others into doing it for you?) The less he has developed these capacities, the more likely he is to feel that he lacks them. An added tragedy of his existence is that he may never find out how capable he really could be.

The N person is interested in using his resources to enhance his own joy and growth. Being more self-satisfied, he consequently has more to give in his relation-

ships with others. The T person, in contrast, abuses
himself. He acts in ways that are ungratifying, destructive, and frustrating to himself. His self-poisoning
patterns often have a compulsiveness about them; it
is as if the person were unable to control these patterns regardless of his awareness of the consequences.
For example, obese people go on eating splurges fully
aware that their momentary gratification will not at all
counterbalance the self-contempt they will feel later.

The N person is organized, is more integrated, and
functions with greater unity toward his objective. The
T person's energies are more diversified and disor-
ganized, with the result that he functions at a marked
disadvantage. Being already dissipated, his stability is
more tenuous, and he is vulnerable to new toxic
encounters and experiences.

EVERYTHING IS RELATIVE

All behavior is a matter of degree; we are never
wholly nourishing or wholly toxic. Jamming our thinking into categories is the source of many toxic attitudes. Any kind of behavior—for example, honesty—
not only is relative but fluctuates widely within the
same person, depending on circumstances and needs.
To label a person as "honest" or "dishonest" is to insist
on placing him in an artificial box. For example, how
honest a person is depends upon the situation in
which he is functioning. A bank teller may be compulsively honest when working at his job, but if he
finds a wallet full of money on the street he may or
may not return it intact to its owner.

Categorical thinking is a self-imposed enslavement
that oppresses the person with value judgments, and

it is extremely toxic in relationships with one's self and the world. The person is always stuck (or sticking others) with "labels."

A human being and his behavior are a *process*, in which change is constantly occurring. We can modify our behavior in ways of our own choosing. Change or growth does not imply that we must make our self over or that the "bad" or "diseased" part of our self must be eliminated as if by surgery.

Toxic attitudes begin when a person imposes, or clings to, unrealistic restrictions on himself on some basis other than his own self-regulating processes. No one gets everything his own way, and toxic processes are an inevitable aspect of living. It is our own responsibility to choose what toxic influences we will submit to and what toxic intrusions we will reject. Nourishing growth and change involve movement in which various potentials are developed or diminished according to our ongoing needs. The more we can appreciate our own ability to change, the greater the possibilities for experiencing our own aliveness. Sometimes we deliberately seek contrast as an enriching kind of experience. When we are enmeshed in a life style of pressure and activities, we yearn for a vacation of idleness and rest. When we are restless with unused energy, we may feel a desperate urgency to become involved in something exciting.

Routine and unvarying human behavior deadens us. To be alive involves variation in attitudes and behavior patterns. Contrast lends our experiences a feeling of intensity and vitality. Our willingness to experiment with various attitudes and behavior patterns helps us avoid the chronic poisoning of a dull routine.

Nourishment and toxicity tend to be mutually exclu-

sive. A person functioning in a nourishing manner is
necessarily being less poisonous at the same time. Conversely, when his behavior is largely poisonous, he
tends to minimize his ability to be nourishing.

Adjustment is an ongoing, creative process of being
and becoming. The development of our awareness is
the process through which we discover who we are
and what we wish to become. We never lose this
potential, regardless of age or the stagnating power
of past experiences. Remarkable reversals are increasingly possible as we become more aware of our toxic
attitudes. We all have the potential to move away
from a T orientation and toward a predominantly N
orientation. We can all become more nourishing and
enjoy ourselves and others and also react to our pain
and frustration more effectively. We can discover how
to exist in greater harmony with ourself and our
environment. We can discover more of our inner aliveness and become more capable of self-expression.
In the process we discover our givingness, lovingness,
and creativity: we discover our nourishing self.

CHAPTER TWO

Antidotes to Toxic Behavior

THE GROUND RULES FOR ANTIDOTES TO TOXIC LIVING

The following series of statements reflects the most effective orientation for discovering antidotes to toxic experiences. When we acquire such an attitude, we are best able to fulfill our potential for a nourishing life.

1. It is my responsibility when I poison myself or allow others to poison me.
2. It is my responsibility to discover antidotes to minimize these toxic experiences.
3. It is my responsibility to discover *how* I poison myself and *how* I allow others to poison me.
4. It is my responsibility to be aware of how I relate to others in ways that are poisonous to them.
5. My well-being (or the lack of it) is in my own hands, and I will not avoid this by acting helpless and expecting others to give me what I need.

6. I will not immobilize myself (cop out) by insisting that the world has been unfair and "owes me."

7. When other people abuse or manipulate me, I will do what I can to prevent this rather than waste my energy demanding that *they* be different.

8. I recognize that many of my needs depend on my relationships with others, but I will not use this as an excuse for continuing in poisonous relationships.

9. I would rather face my fears of emptiness and loneliness by letting go of a toxic person than subject myself to a chronically poisonous relationship.

10. I recognize that my own power to assert myself and take my stand is the best antidote to the toxic influences of the world in which I live.

11. I will seek antidotes in the here and now rather than blaming past experiences and relationships or waiting for the "right moment" to mobilize myself.

12. I believe that I can more effectively discover for myself what my solutions and antidotes are than anyone else in the world could possibly do for me.

Each of us can stay alive only by assimilating what we need from what is available within our life. When we are able to adequately obtain this necessary nourishment, we survive and flourish. When we become ineffective in this process, our deprivations lead to disintegration and death. Consequently, it is essential that each of us protect ourself from the aggression of others who would, in one way or another, devour us in their quest for survival.

On the physical level, these realities are perhaps more acceptable and more obvious. Yet the same condition exists with respect to our need for emotional self-preservation. We must discover how to become an effective self-nourisher and how to have nourishing relationships with others. We must also discover how to minimize our own self-poisoning behavior as well as how to protect ourself from the toxic intrusions of others.

Regardless of a toxic person's reasons (excuses) when he fails to provide himself with adequate emotional nourishment, he commits psychic suicide, since he weakens his ability to satisfy his own needs and at the same time becomes increasingly vulnerable to attack. The only valid issue is whether a person chooses to do the best he can to stay alive or whether his personal existence—for selfish or altruistic reasons —is of secondary importance to him.

On the psychic level, a commitment to personal survival includes concern for others. For N people this attitude simply acknowledges that their emotional nourishment depends not only on their ability to nourish themselves but also on relating to others in a nourishing way. At the same time, the nourishing person is aware that everyone is continually in actual or potential contact with the toxic patterns of others as well as those within himself. We live in a social and physical environment that contains a great variety of toxic elements.

The antidotes to toxic experiences begin with our interest in actually discovering ways to avoid toxic experiences or to minimize their effects. This we can do most directly and effectively by concentrating on the present as it unfolds day by day, even moment by moment. It is fantasy for a person to believe he can commit himself to seeking a less toxic existence in the same way he would announce his dedication to some religious doctrine. Rather, his commitment must be to a continued and increasing awareness of how he *is* poisoning himself or allowing himself *to be* poisoned. Once he begins this process, he can then do his best to counteract these experiences.

When toxic patterns are sufficiently minimized, nourishing ones naturally emerge. The potential for their discovery exists always. Once we begin to experiment for ourselves, we will find our own therapeutic potentials (antidotes). They exist within each person on the psychic level in the same way that antibodies on the physical level ward off disease. In essence, the entire process of remedying toxic patterns rests on minimizing their poisonous effect sufficiently to allow the organism's inherently nourishing potentials to prevail. In the end, each person "gets well" on his own, or he doesn't get well at all.

Attitudes and behavior patterns are toxic when they interfere with our self-regulating processes. Antidotes include any experience that helps to counteract those behavior patterns which disrupt our natural flow. Toxic experiences also include activities that are meaningless, waste our time and energy, or elicit unpleasant or painful reactions without any present or anticipated gratification. Thus, being annoyed at a boring conversation, a restless feeling of not knowing what to do with oneself, or a feeling of irritation when someone is late for an appointment is a signal of a toxic experience.

We may be fully aware of a recurring toxic experience and yet decide to do nothing about it. It is our responsibility to choose when and how we will react. It is not assumed that remedial action is always necessary or that we necessarily want to take any action. For reasons of our own, we may choose to continually involve ourself in activities and relationships that we know are toxic. There is no implication that we "should" change our life—the choice is ours.

Peggy certainly loved Paul deeply. She would often jokingly say to their friends that her willingness to put up with his peculiarities indicated how much she loved him. Actually, Paul was not so much peculiar as he was absolutely rigid on certain convictions and practices which, as he put it, "My father and his father before him believed in deeply." While they joked about it to their friends, it really wasn't funny to Peggy or their three children when Paul would roust them out of bed at six each morning for half an hour of calisthenics. He would tolerate no excuse other than a convincing physical illness. He totally refused to discuss the matter and considered his wife's and children's opinions irrelevant. His toxic attitude was obvious in his refusal to allow his family any self-expression. Nor would he consider any compromise. He held to his rigid rule even with his oldest son, who was a four-letter athlete and only a junior in high school.

In an intimate relationship, respect for the convictions of the other person is no excuse for allowing him to violate one's own integrity.

The more nourishing a relationship, the greater the
likelihood that one person will tolerate those toxic
aspects of the other's behavior about which he can do
nothing. In the same sense, the more caring and emotional involvement we feel, the greater our willingness
to tolerate the toxic behavior of another person. In
contrast, in superficial relationships our willingness to
tolerate toxic interaction is far less.

Alleviating toxic experiences centers on differentiat-
ing what is nourishing and meaningful from what is
ungratifying or destructive to our well-being. The task
is greatly simplified by the fact that once we become
willing to look, our real needs are obvious. Antidotes
themselves begin by focusing on the obvious. It is
obvious that if we are going to seek a more nourishing
existence, we must first be *interested* ("This is important to me") in discovering the nourishing and toxic
qualities of our own behavior.

This process is simple, but it is not easy. Each of us
carries a lifetime of habits and conditioning with
which we distort or avoid the obvious in the here and
now.

It is our responsibility to be aware that our responsiveness is to *this person* and the present
situation rather than past relationships and
earlier irrelevant experiences.

Most of us seek to survive by protecting ourselves in ways that evoke the least amount of stress. The ongoing issue for each of us is what attitudes and behavior are still appropriate and necessary. Many attitudes and behavior patterns are toxic because they represent a continued defense against threats that no longer exist. Whenever this is the case, the person's lack of awareness and persistent wasting of his energy on such obsolete responses is a self-poisoning process.

> Throughout his childhood, Grant would cringe with fear whenever his father yelled at him. He knew he was about to have his ears boxed (literally). He would crouch with his hands over his head, hopelessly trying to protect himself from the dreaded onslaught.
>
> Grant grew to be six feet five inches tall and weigh two hundred sixty pounds, yet whenever someone was angry at him—even his wife—he still felt the same fear; his body tightened, and he assumed a posture of protecting himself from a forthcoming blow.

Continuing to surrender to our phobias only intensifies their destructive power and enhances their poisonous effect on our well-being.

Most so-called "neurotic" or "psychotic" conditions consist largely of an excessive accumulation of obsolete behavior patterns that are so taxing they significantly disrupt the individual's ability to function effectively in the here and now. Similarly, the façades, games, and manipulations each of us (including N people) has adopted are often protective devices learned in the past which are not relevant to the present.

Antidotes involve our interest in deciding whether the energy we expend protecting (squeezing) ourselves against our fears and anxieties is realistic in terms of the present. Whenever we discover that an existing attitude or behavior pattern has become obsolete, we can then seek an antidote by experimenting with other attitudes or behavior to replace the toxic pattern.

Without awareness, a person will persist in repeating a toxic behavior pattern endlessly despite his best intentions.

Arnold knew only too well how painful his loneliness was. Yet he was totally unaware of how he avoided contact with people. He joined a lodge in an effort to overcome his loneliness—yet consistently arrived late for meetings, seated himself in a corner of the room, said nothing, and left hastily at the close of each meeting. A fellow member would have had to all but tackle him in order to make contact. Arnold was totally unaware of his elusiveness and the obvious manner in which he protected himself from his dread of further rejection. He insisted that it just "kept happening"—that he was always unavoidably detained before each meeting and had something urgent to attend to afterward.

Any antidote for loneliness rests on our willingness to explore what we might be doing to isolate ourselves or drive other people away.

In addition to their poisonous effects, toxic patterns tend to contaminate existing nourishing attitudes. No matter how excellent our emotional health, none of us is immune to the poison of toxic experiences.

All antidotes to toxic behavior rest on our individual potentials. We discover reality as soon as we begin using these potentials to gain greater awareness of our sensory data. Any toxic attitude or behavior pattern is potentially responsive to remedial efforts if we "listen" to our experiences with all our various sensory apparatus. The body responds to psychological toxicities just as it does to chemical poisons. Toxic experiences normally elicit a feeling of being damaged. In numerous ways, the body sends messages—some subtle, some urgent—about the need to reject what is experienced as toxic. These sensory messages range from feelings of irritation, annoyance, or boredom to anger, rage, and suicidal depression. As the toxic experience becomes increasingly frustrating, the body presses more intensely for a counterreaction. If we ignore or refuse to take action in response to the increasing demands of our body, an explosive reaction, a psychological symptom (e.g., neurosis), or a psychosomatic breakdown of some body function or organ will occur.

There are three essential areas of relating, none of which can be sacrificed or avoided without producing a lopsided pattern of functioning or eliciting other toxic reactions:

1. A human being *needs* to relate to himself (intra-psychic needs).
2. He *needs* to relate intimately to others (inter-psychic needs).
3. He *needs* to relate to (discover a harmony with) his physical and less intimate social environment.

Many toxic patterns involve denial of, rebellion against, or failure to respond to all three areas of need.

Bill was a graduate student in pharmacology who returned from the Army disillusioned by man's inhumanity to man. "I feel trapped in this system. I don't see any way out but to get an education so I can earn a decent living. I don't feel like being a martyr and I do enjoy material things": This was his explanation for continuing graduate school after his discharge. "I wish I could afford to just drop out," he would laughingly say.

Then it happened: the proverbial rich uncle left him an inheritance of seventy-five thousand dollars. The day Bill received this unbelievable news was the last day he attended classes. He bought a working farm and looked forward to a life of freedom, avoiding submission to society, and expressing his love for his fellow man. His excitement reached an even higher pitch when his friends suggested they form a commune and enjoy the good life together. Each one would take responsibility for doing his share of the work without being ordered about by someone else, and each one would be free to express himself in whatever creative ways he could discover. Bill and eight others arrived loaded with books on farming and an enormous sense of adventure. They were the advance guard; about twenty more were due after the spring semester. All were determined not to allow any kind of authoritarian structure to hamper them.

The spring planting went well, and with the arrival of the others, the commune of thirty was off to a sound start. Everyone was eager to work. They hoped to grow enough food to feed themselves, to cover the cost of maintaining the equipment, and to carry them through the winter.

The initial problem developed when deer and other wildlife began to eat the budding shoots. Those who had labored hardest on the crops were the most upset. They immediately wanted to erect barbed-wire fences and to consider methods of exterminating the offending rabbits and gophers. The other commune members were indignant. After all, hadn't they wanted to live in a commune to escape cruelty and killing? The argument lasted for hours and was resumed again the following night and the night after that. As the frustration grew, some people threatened to leave, while others wanted to elect a neutral person to make the decision. This was shouted down as the creation of a new authority—and they would have no part of that! Nothing was resolved, and a large portion of the crop was destroyed.

Those working in the vegetable patches now seemed less energetic. In September and early October the remaining crops were harvested and preparations were made for the winter. Cash from the sale of the surplus was much less than had been anticipated. Some needed warm clothing; others needed medical care, and one member had to be hospitalized. Bill paid these bills, hoping to recoup the money later. The "nonviolent group" who had opposed exterminating the rodents were becoming more vociferous in their demand that the commune become wholly vegetarian. This would stop the killing of animals and would simplify their food requirements. Others insisted that if they were willing to do the work of raising chickens, they had a right to eat them if they wanted to. The disagreements began to fester and the feelings of harmony to fade. The winter was severe, and the group grew increasingly bored and irritated with one another. They had no money for luxuries such as entertainment. In addition, the main pump broke down and Bill had to advance another fifteen hundred dollars to repair it. By February, eleven members had left. In the spring, the rest began again to plant crops, for another try.

Now their friends began showing up in increasing numbers—some out of curiosity, some just for the summer, others sincerely interested in joining the group. Mostly they were in the way; and while they were available and willing to work, they actually did very little. No one was turned away, since this would be considered uncaring and greedy. They planted a larger crop, and hopes soared that things would be better. Conflicts among the members continued to arise and —since the nonauthoritarian attitude was inviolable—were individually resolved, repressed, or avoided. When the stress became too much for any individual, that person usually left the commune.

Without the enthusiasm of the previous year, things were not going well at all. The inefficiency and disorganization were becoming increasingly obvious. The group insisted that each person must handle his own conflicts with other individuals the best way he could and that no group decision would be enforced against the personal feelings of some members of the group.

Their second-year crop was an abysmal failure. It was obvious that they could not survive the winter on what they had grown. Bill too had become increasingly disillusioned and disheartened. His funds had been depleted repairing equipment and meeting other necessary expenditures to keep the farm going. When several members suggested that he again lend money for the winter provisions, he exploded. There was no alternative now but for the commune to dissolve. Everyone left except Bill and three others.

The next spring Bill had to mortgage the farm for seed, supplies, and hired labor. The hired laborers produced fully three times as much work per day as any of the commune members had ever done, and at a minimal wage. Bill also managed to subdue his guilt at the relief he felt in eliminating the rodents which had eaten most of his previous two crops. Those who came to visit that summer met with a cold reception: "I'm in no mood to socialize or be idealistic. My back's against the wall, and if I don't produce a cash crop this year, I'm going to lose the farm."

Bill's noble, altruistic endeavor, while well

meant, was doomed to failure. The idea that a group can survive without a social structure was only one of his toxic illusions. His rebelliousness against society, combined with a lack of any reasonable alternative plan, was doomed to have its toxic effect on each individual member.

Self-expression that ignores reality and the consequences of individual action produces only chaos.

When a person expresses his givingness by allowing others to suck nourishment at his expense, he not only poisons himself but invariably ends up exhausted and with nothing further to give.

The willingness to be selective and limiting in giving is essential for survival.

ANTIDOTES AS PROCESS

To initiate any antidote process, we must be aware of what is happening that is toxic and then discover how the toxic pattern is perpetuated. Brief, one-shot toxic episodes are of less significance than those arising in ongoing relationships. Effective action against these poisonous patterns is to be discovered in antidote *processes* rather than in a single decisive action (or series of actions) that the person hopes will bring about an end to the toxic pattern once and for all. The discovery of an antidote means that it is then available to the individual to be utilized "as needed."

The antidote *process* can be stated as follows: "What can I do (or stop doing) when it is obvious that I am continually exposed to a recurring toxic pattern in a situation or relationship that I am not willing to terminate?"

A poisonous attempt at an antidote process can be stated as follows: "What can I do (or stop doing) to put an end to this toxic pattern *once and for all* when I am unwilling to terminate the relationship or avoid the situation?"

Many people who earnestly seek antidotes to the toxic elements in their lives end up poisoning themselves further in their search for a remedy.

THERAPIST: What do you do when you get angry at your wife?

JOHN: I overcame that a long time ago. Anger is childish. When you get angry you just make a fool out of yourself. If I don't like something, I wait until I've thought the problem out, and then we sit down and discuss it calmly like two civilized human beings. The problem is, my wife keeps getting emotional. I can't stand it when she raises her voice or starts to cry. I've told her this repeatedly, and she still does it; she says she tries to stay calm but can't help herself. I've solved that problem, too: when she begins to get emotional, I leave and go for a walk.

THERAPIST: So what's the problem that brought you here for a consultation?

JOHN: It's about my wife. Lately, for some reason, she is increasingly irritable. She's totally unreasonable and even refuses to try to discuss things with me.

In intimate relating, attempting to change the
other person is a poisonous remedy.

Antidote: I respect your right to be angry in your
own way even though I don't like it. I will handle
my discomfort with your anger instead of trying
to make you different.

John was full of good intentions and meant well
when he decided that suppression of anger was really
an achievement to be proud of. He acted in good
faith when he insisted that his wife also learn to "control" her emotions. Perhaps John and his wife were
fighting in a toxic way, but their attempt to subdue
their emotions only added more stress to their relationship. Apparently John felt he had achieved his
purpose, since his wife no longer "got emotional"—at
least, not in his presence. It is irrelevant that he was
unaware of his poisonous way of relating to her. It is
equally irrelevant that he was mystified by her
increased irritability. Whenever poison is used to
counteract other poison, the toxic effect is cumulative.

To put it differently, the end does not justify the
means. For the means or remedy *is* the very process
through which the relationship improves. The means
is in essence the way in which the two people relate
to each other—how they get what they want, how they
resolve their conflicts, and how they set limits on their
interaction with each other. In the above case, John's
heavy-handed "power play" brought quick results
(achieved its end), but the superficial tranquillity
achieved by means of a toxic manipulation (telling her
how she "should" behave) was only a façade covering

the growing turmoil within her. The art of emotional nourishment includes the awareness of when one's efforts are motivated by another toxic attitude ("I want to end my pain as quickly as possible, no matter how").

RELAX! WE'LL DO IT FOR YOU

At last, modern science has found the answer to man's emotional suffering. No longer does anyone need to feel the pain of anxiety, tension, depression, or futility. It was announced in London yesterday that the well-known psychiatrist Dr. P. T. Barnum, IV, had perfected his "delta-wave apparatus" after twenty years of research. He announced that he has turned the patent rights over to Gimmick Products, Inc., which will mass-produce the apparatus for distribution throughout the world. The process is totally painless, and the person simply switches on the apparatus and sits in front of it for five minutes a day. According to Dr. Barnum, "All anxiety, tension and apprehension fade away." . . .

A brief perusal of newspapers and magazines will reveal that the above example is not all that exaggerated. Countless similar gimmicks, techniques, and "discoveries" are advertised almost every day—but the truth of the matter is that we rarely find antidotes through easy "answers" or quick gimmicks. There are no formulas that are automatically effective antidotes or that can relieve us from active responsibility for doing our best to live a nourishing life.

People who try to *follow* a "prescription of antidotes" end up poisoning themselves with the would-be antidotes. For example, a person who "programs" himself to automatically terminate a relationship as soon as he has a toxic experience is behaving like a robot (irresponsibly): "You are poisonous—I don't want to be poisoned—so goodbye." Since everyone is toxic to some degree, his "mechanical antidote" will inevitably lead to emotional isolation, which is also toxic.

A toxic person is usually unaware of the fact that he himself is the central initiator of his behavior. He projects, denies, or otherwise avoids responsibility for his attitudes and actions. Turning over this responsibility to the "its" and "theys" of the world around him perpetuates the poisoning process.

Even when the poisoning is in reality instigated by others, each of us must accept our responsibility to do what we can to protect ourself from such intrusions.

It is each person's responsibility to discover his own solutions to his self-poisoning patterns and the toxic intrusions of others.

"FIRST, I'VE GOT TO GET MY HEAD ON STRAIGHT"

"I'm just a ding-y chick—I like to make love, turn on, and get my kicks any way I can—I don't know any other way to be—I just want to have fun. Everyone over thirty is screwed." This is how Sandy described herself to her therapist. She had kept the appointment only because her father threatened to cut off her allowance. Sandy was nineteen, an only child whose parents had been

divorced when she was four. Since then each of them seemed to have concentrated on outdoing the other in winning Sandy's favor. Sandy appeared totally uninhibited and would nonchalantly talk to anyone she met as if they were old friends. She behaved as if she just couldn't be bothered to take herself seriously. "I'm a ding-a-ling and that's my bag." Sandy's position was that she simply lacked the capacity to be any different.

The following dialogue took place between Sandy and the therapist at their first session:

THERAPIST: You do your ding-y number very well, and you're very convincing. I don't believe that's all there is to you.

SANDY: *(sarcastically)* Oh, you shrinks say that to everyone.

THERAPIST: *(also laughing at Sandy's comments)* I'm not interested in selling you anything. I'm telling you how I experience you, and I respect your right not to believe me.

SANDY: *(still laughing and not giving up her façade for an instant)* Okay, Doc, do your thing. Psych me out. I can take it.

(Therapist smiles and remains silent. Neither says a word for a full two minutes, while gradually Sandy's persistent smile begins to fade.)

S: This is getting creepy. Can I go now?

T: We have about fifteen minutes before the hour is up, but you can leave any time you wish.

S: You're okay, Doc. But I don't think you can help me.

T: I didn't know you wanted any help. I thought

you were here only because your parents insisted.

S: I don't know. I try not to think about it. I've
always been this way. I don't think I could be
any different.

T: Are you interested in being different, as you put
it?

S: Well, I do know how I come on, and I don't
always like it; I just don't think there's anything
else to me. I've been this way all my life—lighthearted, laughing, never serious, and above all
never letting anybody hurt me.

T: Could you tell me what you mean by not letting
anyone hurt you?

S: Oh, I know what these guys think of me. They're
just after my body. I make a game of it. Sometimes I really like one of them and I would like
to be friends. But I don't know how to do that.
They want to go to bed with me, so I go to bed
with them. When they get tired of that, I don't
see them any more. (*Long pause. A tear begins
to run down Sandy's face.*) Then I get depressed. But there's nothing I can do about it. I
don't dare let anyone see how I feel. I used to
tell my parents when I felt bad and they would
only say, "Oh, don't feel that way" and offer me
some new goodie to take my mind off my troubles. No one takes me seriously. No one even
knows me. I don't think there's anything inside
of me. I don't even know who I am myself. I'm
just not capable of being serious. Maybe it has
something to do with genes: I'm a bad seed.
(*Again laughs.*)

T: You sound like you're some kind of freak—like some human part of you is missing.

S: Right. I'm just freaky like I was born with something missing in my head. Now, don't tell me you can do something about *that*.

T: If you're interested, we could take a closer look at some of your feelings.

S: Well, the folks certainly have the bread, and I certainly have the time. So if you want to, why not?

Discovering antidotes does not mean becoming a different person. Not only is this unnecessary, it is impossible as well. We discover antidotes to toxic behavior through the process of putting into action our unused potentials and resources.

The belief that one is missing some quality ("I can't give! I'm incapable of loving!") is toxic. When a person bemoans the "fact" that he is incapable of love, has never learned how to give, or is unable to sustain intimacy with another person, he is really saying either that he has not discovered his nourishing capabilities or that he has pushed them so far out of his awareness that he is unsure of their existence.

It may be that he was taught as a child that he was not "good enough" and continues to torture himself with his attitude. Or, he hopes that enough achievement, or "success," will give him the feeling that he is acceptable, is lovable, and has a right to have what he needs. The belief that something is "missing" or "bad" ranges from the sophisticated person who feels he must "resolve his neurosis" in order to become a human being to those who torture themselves with futile attempts at redemption.

For some, the solution to living lies in blocking off the conflicts and otherwise seeking to escape the whole problem. They choose to simply survive rather than to adjust by growth and integration. Others seek to cope by a life pattern of struggle against themselves, others, and their environment. Their behavior is manipulative and totalitarian. For them, the byword is "combat." Their principal weapons—and toxicities —are power, control, and a struggle for superiority against what they consider poisonous in themselves, in others, or in their world.

LIVING IN THE NOW

Although it is important to live in the here and now, the concept can be twisted into fantastic distortions. To be unable to anticipate the consequences of our behavior is a sure way to frustrate and poison ourselves. Each of us is responsible for the consequences of his own behavior. Refusing to recognize this reality leads to chaos and alienation. Impulsiveness—living *for* the moment as if there were going to be no tomorrow—is almost invariably toxic.

Sharon's family placed a strong emphasis on intellectual pursuits. Her father was a physicist and worked for a large aerospace company. Her mother had taught graduate courses in journalism and held a Ph.D. in English. Sharon was fascinated with history and politics and wanted a career in the academic world.

She had met Larry two years before he entered the service. It was the beginning of the semester of her senior year when the news came that he had been killed in a "freak accident" while on maneuvers. Sharon went into a deep depression which culminated in an attempt at suicide. She took an overdose of barbiturates and would have died had she not accidentally been discovered.

When she awoke in the hospital, she was furious that they had not let her die. She spent three months in a psychiatric ward before her doctor agreed to discharge her. Her suicidal impulses were replaced by a cynical, bitter, deeply angry attitude toward the world. When her therapist suggested that she continue her studies, she literally laughed in his face: "What the hell for? What's the point of teaching anybody anything when the world is such a crazy place? I'm going to get mine now—I haven't the least intention of living past thirty."

Sharon was still mourning for Larry and furious about the way he had died. She began using drugs, moved in with a group of "dropouts," and started borrowing money from her parents, which she and her friends spent in impulsive splurges, seeking excitement. When her parents protested about this, she responded by promising them she would never ask them for anything again—and she never did. She became involved in a shoplifting ring, which flourished for a year and a half. She was caught while under the influence of drugs, but would have been given probation except for her defiant attitude toward the judge. She was sentenced to prison for one to five years.

Three months after she went to prison, her father suffered a severe heart attack and died. Nineteen months later, Sharon was paroled. Now for the first time since Larry's death she began to feel interested in living. "Coming down" from her impulsive life style of the previous four years was enormously painful. She had a great deal of guilt about her father's death and her mother's sacrifices for her sake. She could not, of course, undo what had been done. She could only accept the present consequences of her past behavior.

Being obsessed with a wasted past does nothing but waste the present. Regrets are an exercise in futility which can go on forever.

Living *in* the moment means experiencing to the fullest what is nourishing in the present. ("Today is the *first* day of the rest of my life.") The essence of living in the now is a continued awareness of our experiencing self. There is nothing impulsive or irresponsible in this attitude. Rather, it emphasizes the reality of living: effective emotional nourishment is possible only in the present.

When "doing your thing" is construed as doing what we choose without being willing to accept the results of our actions, it is a toxic attitude which is apt to result in poisonous behavior both toward ourself and toward others. Each of us must decide whether he cares about himself (and others) and his existence one week from now or ten years from now. One man saves his money to buy a home, while another decides to travel. The only way we can decide which is "better" for us is by accepting full responsibility for the choice and its consequences. When our needs include other people, we must care about their needs, and while the nourishing person cares about other people in general, he is particularly caring toward those with whom he is intimate.

THE STEAMROLLER APPROACH

The opposite of "doing your own thing" is a steamroller attitude toward needs, goals, or aspirations. People with this attitude concentrate only on getting the job done, regardless of its effect on their over-all well-being. T people who function as steamrollers constrict themselves and their lives in order to accomplish their goals. The pain, emotional drain, and other poisonous effects to themselves are considered as largely irrelevant.

In most cases there are more realistic solutions—those involving a compromise between impulsiveness and "grinding it out until it's done." To function effectively in response to one's particular need invariably means that other needs must be at least temporarily suppressed. It is this reality which makes sense out of the word "work" as a necessary and nourishing function. Work implies an effort, an expenditure of energy which we are not entirely willing to make. Work includes energy directed toward suppressing the distractions of secondary needs so that we can focus more fully on our most pressing need at the moment.

More effort is required when the work at hand strongly violates our present needs. In contrast, working on a project we consider meaningful and interest-

ing demands less effort. N people "work" in ways that
are as harmonious as possible with their natural flow
of needs.

Warren was a relentless grinder. Initially, in
his career as a writer, he would work only when
he felt his creative juices were flowing. On such
occasions he would write for hours, while at other
times he would go for days without typing a single word. Usually he would work for a few hours,
then feel burned out and turn to other activities.

After his initial successes, the demand for his
books increased greatly and his publisher was
anxious for new manuscripts. Now Warren began
to regiment himself. He began to set up schedules
and rigidly refused to allow himself to disrupt
them. He was determined to sit at the typewriter
for so many hours each day whether he wrote a
single word or not. His creativity dwindled, and
his productivity along with it. Eventually he
decided to give up his career as an author. He
canceled his contracts with his publisher and
began teaching. Subsequently, much to his surprise, he again discovered the spontaneous flow
of his creativity. He realized that he could work
effectively only when *he* needed to express himself and that he could not force himself to be
creative.

A nourishing attitude (or antidote) about "work"
emphasizes our belief that if we develop at our own
pace—satisfying our needs—we will successfully complete the task. Such a belief eliminates the need for
motivations such as deadlines and other external pres-

sures. If we are willing to confront all the opposing, conflicting needs that divide our energies and concentrate on the most important, we can function effectively and almost effortlessly. The N person realistically confronts his options and makes choices according to his own needs. When an N person feels in conflict about what choice to make, he allows himself to flow with these inner needs as he experiences them. If he is restless and unable to concentrate on a task, and feels the need for exercise, he is willing to shift his attention to the latter need first. This *is* his inner reality—his most pressing need at the moment. Furthermore, when his need for exercise has been satisfied, the energy used to suppress it is then available to increase his attention on the work at hand. People who refuse to risk experimenting with this kind of antidote to their work problems often lack trust in themselves and are fearful that following the flow of their own needs will simply lead from one self-indulgence to the next.

Undoubtedly, most of us would rather play in the sand, paint a picture, or watch television than sit down to do our laundry or income-tax returns. Those who are wealthy rarely discipline themselves to do a dull, tedious job—they simply hire someone else to do it for them. It is a nourishing attitude, and one with enormous antidote potential, to minimize the tedious, boring chores of life in whatever way is possible. The luckiest among us are genuinely fascinated with the way in which they must earn a living. But even when we are faced with a disagreeable job, we can still choose whatever work at the moment seems most appetizing or least distasteful. Staying in touch with one's flow of needs and being responsive to them is in essence an attitude of commitment to oneself to minimize toxic endeavors and to lessen the poisonous effects of the demands of unpleasant tasks that must be done.

NOURISHING AND TOXIC RISK-TAKING

Each of us must inevitably take risks if we are to respond to our needs for self-expression or reach out to the environment for what we want. Risk is inherent in this process (rather than event). Since various needs (deprivations) arise in a more or less continuous sequence, N people have a continuity about their risk-taking activities. This process is apt to be most nourishing and effective when we are willing to make contact primarily on the basis of our own needs and our own willingness (or lack of it) to take risks.

> Joanne was feeling very good about herself. She had just returned from a delightful summer away from the city; in addition, she had lost the fifteen pounds she had so much wanted to get rid of. She heard that Ralph had broken up with his girl friend during the summer. She decided to call him and say hello (take a risk), even though she was fearful he might not be interested in her.

Toxic risk-taking, on the other hand, frequently takes the form of a "program":

> Betty had just moved into an apartment building that rented exclusively to single people. One of the features that attracted and frightened her

was the social-activities room where people congregated informally every evening. A month before moving in, Betty had resolved to "make herself" spend her very first evening socializing: "Come hell or high water, I'm going to stay in that room with those people for at least two hours."

The movers had come at eight A.M. and left at three P.M. By seven o'clock, Betty was exhausted trying to get things in order. She was depressed, irritated, and anxious. Her best table had been badly scratched, and several small items were missing. Her brother had promised to help her, but hadn't shown up at all. Nevertheless, she made herself get dressed, and with her head high and her shoulders back, she marched down the stairs and into the social-activities room. "You *will* relate; you *will* be cheerful, outgoing, and friendly," she told (programmed) herself. She pushed away her urgent need for sleep and the little voice inside her timidly suggesting that perhaps she would be more willing to take this risk the following evening. She behaved in a forced, mechanical way, as if she *had* to perform. Later she learned that the other people present experienced her as a "boring phony who was trying too hard."

Resolutions and programs cut off the healthy self-regulating processes that are the essence of spontaneous, easy-flowing behavior. They smother spontaneity with deliberate, forced, premeditated behavior. Programming also cuts off the continuity of awareness and the feedback we normally use to regulate our ongoing behavior. It encourages us to ignore both our awareness of what we are experiencing and our awareness of how others are reacting to us.

Forced behavior and deliberateness usually turn other people off in intimate relating.

Enhancing nourishing behavior and avoiding toxic behavior is realistic only when there are reasonable options that do not involve excessively detrimental consequences. A university has *real* power over its students: A student must study if he is to achieve the goal for which he came to school in the first place. If he wants his degree, he must "jump the hurdles" even when he experiences them as time-wasting, boring, or otherwise toxic. He must comply with the curriculum set forth by the university in order to obtain his degree. The nourishing person, however, will try to select the program that offers the most satisfaction.

IT ISN'T ALWAYS EASY

When Leo graduated from high school, he was told bluntly by his father, "I've raised you—provided you with bed and board for eighteen years—and now you're on your own." Leo quickly found a job in an accounting office. At first he did menial chores, but he learned the work rapidly and seemed to have a promising future with the company. His real interest, however, was law, and he was determined one way or another to become a lawyer. He began attending evening courses in a local university. Despite his long hours at the office, he managed to take two or three courses each semester.

He attended school for six years before he had accumulated enough credits to be accepted in law school. Many times during these six years he felt fed up: "I'm really working two jobs—one at school and one at the office. I have no time to enjoy myself. Sometimes I feel like a jerk using up my life trying to reach a goal that I'll probably never make anyhow."

He was finally accepted in the law school and, since he had no financial reserves, had to continue working. The demands of law school were even more taxing. He had to take more units and work at his accountant job late into the evenings. He needed his weekends to study and catch up on his sleep. There was no time for leisure. In addition, the tuition for law school was much higher. He was forced to move to a cheaper apartment and trim every expense to the minimum. Yet he persevered. He knew what he wanted, and he was willing to put up with whatever sacrifices were necessary in order to get it.

One sure way to poison oneself is to expect or seek toxic-free relationships and experiences.

An important antidote in a culture that emphasizes permissiveness is the willingness to accept unavoidable toxic experiences while continuing to seek the gratifications of one's needs. This is particularly true when we undertake an endeavor that involves a considerable length of time and requires a sustained effort to complete.

ONE MAN'S NOURISHMENT IS ANOTHER MAN'S POISON

By "owning" all his attitudes, behavior patterns, and reactions to others, an N person avoids being judgmental. His focus is on what *he* finds fits his needs, what *he* experiences as nourishing or toxic. While he may clearly state what he likes or dislikes, he does not attempt to "sell" his opinions to others by implying that they "should" be like him. The nourishing person does not tell another, "You should not manipulate me." He may say in effect, "I feel manipulated by you." He *owns* how he experiences (and reacts to) the way the other relates to him. In essence, what he says is, "If you feel that what you are doing in our relationship contributes to your well-being or nourishes you, I respect your right to be the way you feel is best for you. However, I experience what you are doing as toxic [manipulative] to me."

The nourishing person expresses how he experiences the other person—he does not pronounce a judgment that he is right and the other is wrong.

He: Let's stop volleying for a while. I think I can show you some pointers that will improve your game.

She: I don't want to stop. I'm enjoying myself. I would like to finish the set.

He: It will only take a few minutes, and I think

you'll find your game will improve quickly. For one thing, you're not holding your racket right . . .

SHE: I don't want a lesson right now. I'm enjoying myself. Come on, let's play—I know I could be better.

HE: Why do you have to be so stubborn? Just try holding the racket the way I suggest.

SHE: You're taking all the fun out of it for me. If you're not enjoying yourself, just say so, and we'll stop. But I don't want a tennis lesson.

HE: God, some people are just ungrateful. I spent years perfecting my backhand and invested hundreds of dollars in lessons and I just want to share it with you, and you won't let me.

SHE: Take all the lessons *you* want; I don't want any.

HE: You're too much. Maybe you ought to see a shrink about your stubbornness.

In the above dialogue, "he" has good intentions. He thinks he has something of value to offer. "She" is enjoying herself (a nourishing experience). He refuses to accept this and persists in his attempts to "sell" her something that will be "good for her" until he frustrates (poisons) himself by refusing to allow her to be exactly the way she wants to be at the moment. In the following dialogue, he avoids selling and being judgmental by owning his feelings about the game.

HE: There are a couple of things about your form which I could point out to you that might improve your game quite a bit.

SHE: I appreciate the offer, but I'm having fun and

enjoying myself right now. I would like to continue the set.

HE: Okay. If you're interested, you can ask me after
we finish and I'll point out a couple of flaws I
noticed in your form.

HE: *(silently to himself)* She doesn't give me a very
interesting game, and she sounds like she's not
interested in becoming a better player. I think
I'll look around for someone else who gives me
a better game.

After the set is finished:

SHE: I really enjoyed that—it was a lot of fun. I
hope you don't mind my lack of enthusiasm
about improving my game.

HE: I appreciate your being honest about it.

SHE: I think I blew it. I'll bet you never ask me to
play tennis again *(laughing)*.

HE: Not necessarily. If I want a more challenging
game, I *will* find another partner. I really like
your openness, and I have a hunch we might
find other things in this world to enjoy with
each other besides tennis.

A particular behavior pattern may be experienced
as poisonous on one occasion and nourishing on
another. Similarly, the same incident may be experienced as nourishing by one person and toxic by
another.

To label what a person does as intrinsically poisonous or nourishing ignores the experience of the individual. A man who is afraid of his anger may withdraw
into a shell to avoid the catastrophe he imagines will

surely follow. Subsequently he may risk expressing his anger more openly and experience this as more nourishing. For him what was toxic is now nourishing.

CONTINUITY OF ACTION

Well-being and growth are a function of the interaction between self and environment. We must constantly take in various kinds of nourishment and expel (or repel) what we find poisonous. Effective functioning is based on our continuous responses to our needs —including our need to withdraw.

While awareness is a prerequisite for change, it remains an incomplete experience when effective responsiveness is lacking. Initiating action in response to the awareness of our needs is an ongoing process. Functioning *is* action. When a person allows himself to become immobilized, he becomes increasingly nonfunctional. Consequently, when we feel stuck in a toxic relationship or situation, it is still our responsibility to initiate whatever action we can to get unstuck ... if in fact that is what we wish. Deciding that a difficulty is insurmountable guarantees a poisonous impasse. When functioning is frozen, frustration inevitably mounts, and emotionally (if not physically) the person begins—however slowly—to die.

OPPORTUNITY KNOCKS . . . AND KNOCKS . . . AND KNOCKS

It is a toxic attitude for anyone to expect to evolve into an "awareness machine" that unfailingly sorts nourishing and toxic experiences and reacts with great promptness and spontaneity. A healthy human being is often inefficient, and frequently slow to become aware—but since most self-poisoning patterns recur continually, we all have many opportunities to discover what is poisonous and to search for more effective antidotes.

CONCLUSION

While everyone's N and T patterns are fairly consistent, the possibilities for change are continually present. The potential for diminishing toxic behavior and enhancing nourishing attitudes exists in all of us. The nourishment–toxicity balance is always in flux, always evolving in reaction to how we experience our lives.

An emotionally nourishing life pattern, conducive to growth and integration, is the most fertile soil in which to discover antidotes. Emotional nourishment is the cornerstone on which we develop our potential to resist toxic experiences.

CHAPTER THREE

The Self-poisoner:
Patterns of Self-induced Toxicity

THE DEATH TRAPS OF
AVOIDANCE AND INHIBITION

Self-poisoning processes can kill. Some of the most common reasons we avoid being ourselves result from the following attitudes:

1. I would rather inhibit myself than risk the disapproval of others.
2. I would rather inhibit myself than risk feeling guilty.
3. I would rather inhibit myself than risk being embarrassed.
4. I would rather inhibit myself than risk failure.
5. I would rather inhibit myself than risk rejection.
6. I would rather avoid myself than face up to my fears.
7. I would rather avoid myself by projecting my problems onto others.
8. I would rather avoid expressing my resentments and anger and instead turn them inward against myself.

9. I would rather avoid myself than face my feelings of inadequacy.

Each individual, whether he is primarily N- or T-oriented, generates his own brand of psychological poisons with which he toxifies himself. Sometimes a person is aware that he is poisoning himself and decides it is necessary to continue to do so. He may be convinced that this is the best he can do for himself under the circumstances. For example, a man may decide to work two full-time jobs in order to earn enough money to impress his friends and neighbors. He may experience many body warnings: symptoms of fatigue, irritability, nervous tension, etc. His physician may specifically advise him to slow down. It is each person's right to subject himself to whatever poison he judges to be necessary, since he carries out the punishment on himself.

The self-poisoner is more willing to place unreasonable demands on himself and to let one particular need dominate his well-being at the expense of other important needs. It does not matter at all whether he is aware of what he is doing to himself or oblivious to his self-poisoning processes. Generally, the self-poisoner lacks awareness of how toxic his attitudes and behavior are to himself. Yet lack of awareness does not lessen the reality of the toxic process—just as a person who is suffering from a terminal disease will die, whether he knows he is ill or not. Self-poisoning on the emotional level is frequently quite subtle, and often a person is unaware of its deadliness, but like a constantly high noise level or polluted air, it saps his strength little by little. A continuous self-induced toxic pattern *must* inevitably erode one's health and well-being, however gradual the poisoning process may be. The only unpredictable aspects are when the breakdown will become obvious and what form it will take.

Helen-Louise is a self-poisoner. To others in her world she is a "wonderful person"—always doing things for everyone. She is conscientiously and deeply devoted to her husband and three children.

As she walks into the office for her first consultation, Helen-Louise forces a smile that scarcely covers the pain and tension her wrinkled brow reveals. She sits down struggling to maintain her composure, looks at the doctor, forces another smile, and makes a trite joke about needing to talk to a head-shrinker. The doctor waits for her to proceed. The silence is too overwhelming; she cannot play her game any longer and bursts into tears. A few minutes later, she begins to talk.

H-L: "I can't stand it any longer. I feel like I'm being used up by my family. They always want something from me. I never have a moment's peace. Every time I talk to my husband, one of the children breaks into the conversation. They even barge into our bedroom and insist on being there with us. My husband feels too guilty to say anything about it. I can't stand the looks on their faces when I tell them that their father and I want to be alone. My son is constantly demanding something. As soon as I do one thing for him, he is after me to do something else. They keep me so busy I no longer have any time to do what I want to do. My husband and I have no chance to talk, and I feel we are growing apart. Lately, I find myself resisting his sexual advances, and I don't understand it at all—I love my husband. Yet I know I'm becoming increasingly irritated with him and the children. I feel very guilty when I find myself wishing the children were all grown up so that I could be alone with my husband. I know they love me, but I'm beginning to resent everyone and everything in that house—as if it were poison. Sometimes I feel as if I'll die if this keeps on."

The "problem" that Helen-Louise brought to the psychologist's office is a case in point. While she lived within the potentially nourishing atmosphere of a family that loved and cared about one another, she poisoned herself by playing "victim" to the toxic manipulations of her children. The fact that she was unaware of the deadly games in which she participated did not make their toxic effects any less devastating to her well-being and her ability to nourish both herself and her family.

A basic attitude toward relieving our self-poisoning patterns is a willingness to say "yes" to what we want and "no" to what we don't want.

The victim of self-induced toxic patterns exists in a state of "dis-ease." T patterns can be compared to emotional and physical health, so the suffix "itis" has been added to many of the words used in this chapter to describe different toxic patterns. The term implies that some poisonous phenomenon is occurring that is destructive to the person.

A person's constellation of toxic behavior includes one or more dominant patterns in addition to others of secondary importance. These self-poisoning patterns can contaminate others. They vary in their infectious qualities as do physical diseases: some are highly contagious and therefore are dangerous; others are relatively noninfectious and not as hazardous.

BEING OTHER-ORIENTED

It is a common self-poisoning attitude of T people to place their emotional security and self-esteem in the hands of others. Their well-being tends to depend primarily on the reactions of other people toward them. Toxic patterns that reflect this attitude are described as other-oriented.

Each person is the most important person in the world to himself and is the center of his own existence.

The poisonous other-oriented attitude is inevitable when a person gives over his power to others and thereby surrenders his freedom to be his self.

APPROVALITIS

This other-oriented pattern of behavior detours the person away from personal growth and an increasing sense of identity. The victim of approvalitis loses the power to regulate his well-being and self-esteem. He impedes his spontaneous self and his search for satisfaction and growth by "psychic stop lights" which he creates in the form of powerful others who might object to his attempts at self-determination. He subjugates himself to a pattern of behavior reflecting the identity and needs of other people instead of his own. He poisons himself with the haunting possibility that someone else might not approve of his actions—a concept he feels would be catastrophic.

Wally lived his life like a politician seeking votes. His creed was: "If you can't say something nice and pleasant, don't say anything at all." When someone spoke to him, he smiled automatically, while continuously nodding his head as if in agreement with whatever was being said. In his social life, he rarely said no to an invitation and generally could be expected to go along with the crowd. Consequently, his friends developed a habit of informing him of their plans assuming that he would be his agreeable self—which he always was.

At the office, he was affectionately nicknamed "Smiley." His willingness to be helpful and to please seemed unlimited. He was easily manipulated by his fellow employees. A pat on the back was all he needed.

His behavior in the privacy of his home was quite a different matter. There he behaved like a bully. He dominated his wife and children and severely criticized them at the slightest provocation. No one outside his home would have believed that this was the same man they worked with or enjoyed socially. The privacy of his home was the only area of his life in which he allowed himself any expression. He was entirely unaware of his self-poisoning pattern, in spite of the fact that he had migraine-type headaches and chronic hypertension, which he used as excuses for his tyrannical behavior toward his family. While still in grade school, his three children had already developed the same timid reactions to disapproval. They were already characterized by their teachers as "ideal, beautifully behaved children whose parents should be proud of them."

Wally needed to discover his own antidotes by realizing that allowing himself to be taken for granted by playing "doormat" or "nice guy" remedied nothing. By ignoring his own integrity (self-respect) and encouraging others to freely dump their demands on him, he continued to be a self-poisoner.

When the victims of approvalitis of one generation become parents, they tend to dominate their children in the same manner in which they were dominated as children. This cycle of chronic infection is typified in families in which each generation is obsessed with controlling and dominating the next generation.

Approvalitis leads to chronic self-immobilization when the person consistently represses all independent action for fear it might incur disapproval from other people. Instead, the victim awaits his cues about what he should do and how he should act. He vainly hopes that if he is good enough, he will gain the approval, nourishment, and gratification he has so long sought. Since at best these rewards are only sporadically conferred by others, the person grows steadily more desperate. At the height of his desperation, the effect of this T pattern may reach the intensity of a homicidal —or suicidal—rage. The toxicity gradually takes its toll, and the victim may even begin to literally look and act as if all the life had gone out of him. He has burned himself out hoping and waiting.

As long as a person continues to postpone living his own life, waiting to be "graduated" by earning the stamp of approval of another, he continues to poison himself.

APPRECIATIONITIS

People who suffer from this toxic pattern feel compelled to constantly do good deeds and favors for others. In turn, other people are supposed to appreciate them and respond. Typically, these people "keep records" on who owes them what. The self-poison comes when the other person simply accepts and enjoys what is given him but doesn't show his appreciation by "paying off." If the T person then demands payment, he is apt to be angrily rejected.

Betty Jean was a very giving young woman who believed that "You don't say no to your friends and family." She was quite open about her attitude and was always available when someone needed a favor. What she kept hidden was her expectation that others should have a similar attitude toward her. She was firmly convinced that when she asked for a favor, she had every right to expect her friends to joyfully comply, regardless of how inconvenient or difficult it might be for them to give her what she wanted at the moment. Whenever she met with a rejection, she would angrily terminate the relationship. Her final words usually were "I'm glad I found out about you—some friend you turned out to be."

In intimate relating, nobody *owes* anybody anything. On the basis of our own willingness and desire to give, each of us must decide when, how, and in what ways we are willing to respond to another.

EXPLANATIONITIS

The T person toxifies himself with his constant need to explain himself and justify his behavior to others. These explanations and justifications bog him down and hamper his freedom to act decisively. Explanationitis ranges from meek defensiveness to belligerent defiance. The victim torments himself by seeking to justify or excuse his every action. The hook in this self-torture game is the importance the person places on other people's understanding and accepting the "whys" of his attitudes and actions. Since one rarely finishes explaining himself, this T pattern becomes an endless barrier to free-flowing self-expression and spontaneity of action.

This is a dialogue between an explainer and her inquisitor:

JOHN: I want to make love to you.

MARY: I like you, but I don't feel I know you yet. I'd like to take more time for us to get acquainted.

J: Why can't we get more acquainted by making love?

M: *(Somewhat flustered)* I just don't feel ready for it yet. Sex is too important to me to take lightly.

J: How long do you have to know me before you'll be ready?

M: I don't know.

J: I thought you liked me.

M: I do like you as a person, but I don't feel ready to go to bed with you.

J: If there's something that bothers you about me, I wish you'd tell me what it is.

M: It's nothing like that—I can't make you understand. . . .

J: Well, I don't feel you've given me any reasonable explanation.

M: I've tried to tell you how I feel about it.

J: Are you always this slow in making up your mind about going to bed with a guy?

M: I'm not trying to be difficult; I just need a little more time. . . . I wish you would understand that.

J: I still don't feel you've given me any satisfactory explanation.

M: I'm feeling more and more pressured by you. I feel like you're putting me on the spot.

J: Okay. I'll have to reach my own conclusion—you just don't like me.

M: Please don't feel that way. That's not true.

J: I don't know what else to think. Maybe we shouldn't see each other for a while.

M: I guess I spoiled things. I'm sorry.

J: Well, you can make it right if you really want to.

M: I don't know what to say—I don't want you to think I'm a prude. . . . I guess I don't have any really good reason not to go to bed with you.

Justifying or explaining *why* one feels as one does is a self-poisoning pattern when it involves personal choices about how one wants to relate to another person.

NICE-GUY-ITIS

A classic self-poisoner is the person who is primarily interested in maintaining his image of "nice guy." His characteristic role reflects his attitude that the most important thing in the world for him is to avoid incurring the displeasure of others by being consistently pleasing, accommodating, and selfless. Beneath this "wonderful person" façade is the spiteful brat who wants his own way and resents his superaccommodating attitude. The "nice guy" (or "nice girl") invariably suffers from a combination of the patterns discussed above. The self-poisoning comes when he refuses to say no and functions, instead, as if he had a phobia about rejecting anyone. When one chronically denies one's self, the inevitable consequence is slow death.

BEING THE "BEST"

All comparison games are toxic. The drive for achievement and "success" is a major toxic pattern with strong cultural sanctions. The compulsion to excel creates an attitude of hostility and estrangement toward others and tends to trap the person into a limited, narrow focus on one aspect of his existence. The effect is further intensified by his neglect of other needs and potentials that must be fulfilled if he is to develop into a complete, integrated person.

Perhaps the most deadly of the comparison games is the one in which the person decides he must be the very best. Once he succeeds, his success is a trap: he has a "reputation," which he must live up to. He poisons himself by functioning as if he had no choice but to maintain his image.

Some people poison themselves by creating idealized images which they hope will prop up their shaky identities. The "swinger" tries to convince the world that he is rejection-proof and that he is never lonely, frightened, or burdened with feelings of inadequacy. This is similar to the "Marine Sergeant image"—of a man who is so tough he can take anything without even feeling shaken.

Sustaining any idealized image drains the person's energies away from his pursuit of broader experiences and fulfillment of other needs. The self-poisoning effect of attaining (and maintaining) an idealized image is inherent in the simple fact that it is not a natural way of being. It is inevitably a façade. Stuck with his comparison game, he finds his only satisfaction in subduing each opponent who appears on the scene to challenge his position. All the while he is aware of the obvious: sooner or later he will be dethroned. The more of his life energy he has invested in this goal, the more poisonous the effect of the dead end of achieving being the "best."

Often when we feel that we must prove ourselves, we are really attempting to compensate for deeper irrational feelings of insecurity and inadequacy.

PERSONAL PERFORMERITIS

"Record-keeping" is particularly poisonous when a person constantly compares himself with himself. Usually, he has a mental progress chart that is part of his poisonous onward-and-upward demand for continual improvement. The greater his need to prove himself in this way, the more toxic he becomes. The poisoning effect of performeritis is increased by the person's uncertainty of how good he really is. The standards he sets for himself, measured against what he imagines to be the capabilities of others, are merely the product of his own fantasies. He is trapped on a self-improvement treadmill.

A woman became upset whenever she felt she was not the most attractive female in the room. She rejected the friendship of women whom she saw as rivals. Typically, her women friends were older, overweight, or in some other way clearly less attractive than she. She subjected herself to a lifelong beauty contest at the expense of enjoying her over-all growth as a person. The process became even more deadly when combined with her morbid fear of growing older. She fantasized diminishing attention and admiration from men as an overwhelming catastrophe.

A similar toxic pattern occurs in aging men who become anxious about their virility. Toxic performeritis often begins to affect their sexual behavior, in that they feel compelled to prove their sexual prowess at the expense of the experience itself. Any relationship is poisoned to the degree to which it is contaminated by preoccupation with performance. In T people of both sexes, anxiety about aging tends to take on an obsessive quality. To the extent that the obsession demands the time, energy, and resources of the person, the remainder of his total identity is deprived and disregarded.

While we all may be interested in developing some talent or ability, focusing on these aspirations *at the expense* of appreciating present functioning is toxic. Performeritis postpones gratification to some future time. Most self-nourishment comes from functioning in the now.

THE TOXICITY OF SHAME

The ability to cope with failure is necessary to emotional well-being. The nourishing person sees his "failures" as experiences that he considers part of a learning process.

For the N person, the experience of failure is focused on the act itself: "Yes, I made a mistake, and it won't be my last!"

The N person avoids poisoning himself because he does not believe that his self-esteem is at stake every time he ventures forth in some new endeavor. The T person, on the other hand, perceives failure as a reflection of his worth as a person. For him, failure is a blow to his idealized self and his acceptability as a human being.

I'M NEVER GOOD ENOUGH

Those who poison themselves with embarrassment over their failures tend to fantasize that if they can perform well enough they will finally achieve an adequate sense of self-esteem. Their quest is futile, though, since the standards they arbitrarily select are almost invariably unreasonable, overdemanding, or perfectionistic. Ironically, any outstanding achievement they do experience tends to be viewed as a fluke. Similarly, any real acceptance by another is met with the attitude "He doesn't know what I'm really like, or he'd feel differently." Or the approving person is held in contempt for his low standards.

FAILURITIS

The person who habitually puts himself down may do it subtly or silently, but he always sends this message to others. When he does something well—and often such people are superior in ability—he sprinkles his accomplishment with self-generated poison. He seems to have a phobia about enjoying himself or his achievements. He can be counted on to toxify a compliment from another by pointing out some failure or shortcoming about what he did or how he did it. This is not modesty but rather a deep conviction that he is essentially a failure, so that anything good which happens through his efforts is undeserved or unjustified.

The woman who wins a cake-baking contest may poison her victory by insisting that the other contestants could have done as well as she if they had spent as many years baking cakes as she had.

Awareness of one's own potentials can be very frightening. While failuritis is self-poisoning, it often serves to protect a person from the even more frightening prospect: "What if I give up calling myself a failure, do the very best I can, and I *still* don't make it!" There is a certain security in telling one's self, "I'm really a failure only because I've never tried my very best!"

TOXIC INHIBITING

"Now see what you've done! When will you learn to listen to us and think before you act?" George was raised by a mother and maiden aunt who constantly criticized his behavior. When George was two, his mother ordered his father out of the house, stating that he was a shiftless, irresponsible philanderer who could make his best contribution to his son's development by disappearing. From that moment on, George's mother and aunt dedicated themselves to raising him to be the exact opposite of his father. Every action was scrutinized. His mother and aunt seemed to take delight in their conscientious feeling that all their labors were for George's best interest and that he would appreciate them more as he grew older.

George became a master at self-control. He learned early never to get excited or to anticipate a joyous prospect, since it was always doubtful whether any pleasure could survive his mother's and aunt's endless discussions and debates.

By the time he completed high school, George's entire way of being was one of restraint. There was absolutely nothing casual about him. His dress was immaculate, his hair always perfectly combed, and he walked with the rigid posture of a West Point cadet. With his exacting manner and deeply ingrained perfectionism, he did well in engineering and became a top-notch specialist in research and development. He could spot the slightest flaw in any experimental design and rose rapidly within the large corporation that hired him immediately after he graduated. He continued to live with his mother and aunt, and their weekly routine remained as precise as ever. George rarely dated, since he had adopted the criticalness of his mother and aunt and had himself become quite intolerant of a woman's slightest flaw.

George was thirty when he met Gretchen. He was immediately intrigued that she held a doc-

torate in engineering and was every bit a match
for him and his perfectionism. Gretchen was a
match for George's mother and aunt as well, and
they were unable to prevent the two from marry-
ing. Gretchen took over where George's mother
and aunt left off. George continued to live an
emotionally frozen existence, totally lacking in
spontaneity. He sought psychotherapy because of
a sexual problem that totally mystified him: he
found Gretchen sexually attractive, and yet he
was unable to reach an orgasm. He concluded
his description of his problem to the therapist
with a statement of genuine bewilderment: "I
just can't understand why I can't let go!"

**To frustrate another person at one's own expense
is invariably toxic.**

Many self-poisoning patterns have as their major
characteristic the methodical inhibiting of self-expression. Toxic inhibitions of spontaneity which the person
chooses to apply against himself are based on his
unrealistic, inappropriate fears and anxieties. The
essence of toxic pressure is the *unnecessary* stress it
places on the person. In inhibiting spontaneity and
joy or hope and optimism, he destroys some aspect of
his aliveness and ability to function more effectively.

EMOTIONAL CONSTIPATION

People often apply a generalized pressure against
their need for self-expression. Their lives consist
largely of patterns of suppressions and avoidances.

These patterns can become extreme and lead to visible tremors of the hands or face. The more chronically constipated person may have achieved such control that nothing shows any more. His masklike outer tranquillity is accompanied by an inner volcano of withheld expressiveness. Refusal to release emotional tension creates a chronic pressure which strains the whole organism and may be reflected in body and facial expression. A pattern of hard, deep lines about the face gives the person a tortured look. Or the constipation may be expressed in a tense voice that is unnaturally high-pitched. A tightly clenched, stiff body and eyes in a habitual squint also reflect the general suppressive attitude. The victim is in a constant state of pain of which he himself may become gradually unaware.

In general, the emotionally constipated person cuts off his contact with other people by his lack of self-expression. His restrained energy then can be directed only against himself. The inevitable breakdown of his body is commonly reflected in a psychosomatic illness such as an ulcer. If he still rejects his need to express his feelings and emotions, the trapped energy of his emotional constipation will seek even more toxic ways to discharge itself.

To express one's self *is* to give one's self nourishment.

PSYCHOLOGICAL DIARRHEA

This pattern, although the opposite of emotional constipation, is equally toxic. The afflicted person behaves as if he couldn't hold anything back. He has little tolerance for frustration and must discharge any kind of tension as quickly as possible. In men, this may take the form of premature ejaculation. Verbal diarrhea is seen in people who *must* talk incessantly to reduce their inner tensions. Silence, even for a minute or two, generates an unbearable pressure.

In effect, these people short-circuit a great deal of potential nourishment. Deeply gratifying experiences often require a healthy build-up of tension to a full peak followed by an intense discharge and more complete gratification.

T people are characteristically phobic about pain and have little tolerance for the tension of unfulfilled needs. Because they expect that their needs will not be gratified, it is difficult for them to consider *any* feeling of tension as a pleasurable experience. They are unable to enjoy the delights of anticipating forthcoming gratification and usually have a compulsive need to discharge any tension as soon as they become aware of it.

Gordon was a precocious child of two gifted parents. Both his mother and father had been only children, and each had always been the center of attention. In their marriage, each had little empathy for the needs of the other. Gordon became an added burden for both his parents to tolerate. They were continually "shushing" him and admonishing him for interrupting them. Gordon recalled countless times when he squirmed with anticipation, almost bursting with the need to express himself or share some experience. Occasionally they would express interest in what he had to say, but even then they cut him off abruptly. He grew to adulthood with deep feelings of anxiety when his needs were not immediately satisfied. He had learned that waiting was not only frustrating but futile. He habitually went to lunch at eleven-thirty A.M. and frequently had food brought up to the office in the middle of the afternoon. He became increasingly overweight and yet refused to control his eating. He would become angry and belligerent when, on business trips, his plane was delayed or someone was late for an appointment. A severe marital problem developed when his wife began refusing his constant sexual advances. He not only was outraged, but actually accused her of deliberately tormenting him by withholding sex. In the same way, he became irritated when dinner was not ready to be placed on the table almost immediately when he came home from the office. Any kind of tension was like an unbearable pain.

Tension and frustration are an inevitable part of being alive. To refuse to tolerate such experiences is to deny this reality. Overcoming this toxic attitude often means letting go of the fantasy that life "should" be easy and that frustration is unfair.

CONTROLITIS

People who insist on controlling their environment poison themselves with their "control madness." They are unwilling to express themselves, reach out, or experiment with new ways of being. When in a position of power, they use the power to inhibit others. This pattern is observable in some "old maid" schoolteachers (of both sexes) who, in their need to control, choose to teach the lower grades. Their primary interest is to control and manipulate, and this is easier with younger children.

Another form of controlitis occurs in the person who continually interrupts himself with trivial matters that must be taken care of immediately. Everything must be under control or he can't relax. When someone else is doing something, he typically observes with a scrutinous eye as to whether the person is doing it right (according to him). The bolder poisoners of this type are full of unsolicited helpful suggestions. Those who are more timid squirm with irritation and restlessness as they observe someone doing something differently from their way. They insist on calling the shots, and they torture themselves when they can't.

GRIEVANCE COLLECTORS

Many people seem to have lives in which nourishing experiences are totally missing. Their emotional lives are largely limited to habitual complaints about their misfortunes. During the infrequent periods when they are not focusing on their grievances, they go into trancelike depressions. For them, aliveness is associated with toxic emotional attitudes. It is as if this poisonous behavior had some sweetness—for without it they are lifeless.

An example is the person who reacts with rage when he encounters injustice. As his anger rises, his aliveness returns. The more he feels justified in his anger, the more he glows in self-righteousness. If he is an employer, he may dump his grievances on the mistakes of his employees, but rarely on a customer or someone who has power over him. In other instances, his rage is directed against abstractions such as society, politics, or world problems. He distorts these activities into a pattern of scapegoating and impotent anger so he can feel alive.

The grievance collector feeds on the unpleasant in numerous ways. It becomes his way of life. These are people who become uncomfortable and awkward in joyful, happy situations. They are embarrassed and flustered when confronted with pleasantness.

The pay-off for those who collect grievances is that in so doing they avoid the risk of initiating any spontaneous behavior of their own.

FOREVERITIS

Another popular self-poisoning game evolves from the Judeo-Christian philosophy that we are all born in sin and can only hope and pray for redemption. There is an infinite variety of patterns to this particular game, all of which consist of the central attitude that misery, misfortune, and unhappiness are permanent when they occur and the likelihood of change for the better is at best remote. On the other hand, any state of well-being is considered a temporary interlude before the next catastrophe. When the person feels depressed, he sincerely believes his depression will last forever. If he is a salesman and business is bad, he is convinced he will never again earn a living. If he is rejected once, he is convinced that no one will *ever* love him. Even when he feels contentment, this kind of self-poisoner is on the alert for approaching disaster. If business is good, he hushes up any expression of this fact: why get excited when financial ruin may be just around the corner? When he is involved in an emotionally gratifying relationship, he is certain it will soon deteriorate. After all, he "knows" that the *real* meaning of life is tragedy, misery, and unhappiness.

The refusal to reach out for the joys and excitements of life is frequently a refusal to face the pain of possible disappointments and rejections.

LONELYITIS

The toxic person confuses solitude and loneliness. Often he equates the two and is simply phobic about being alone. He becomes anxious, frequently to the point of panic, at the prospect of spending time by himself. He may compulsively arrange some activity every evening. Anything will do: dining with people who are boring, attending dull lectures, or just finding someone to get drunk with. The toxic effect is usually experienced as a growing syndrome of fatigue, listlessness, and depression. His strength is drained in struggling against his fear of being alone, and he is totally unable to recognize the energy-charging potentials inherent in healthy solitude. Frequently, he locks himself into an empty relationship that relieves his feelings of loneliness but is otherwise without nourishment or meaning. An adult child living with an aging parent is often an example of this form of poison—even while he cries "martyr" or professes deep devotion to the parent. Another common example is the dead marriage in which the partners tolerate each other in a chronic state of misery: at least they are not alone.

Some people poison themselves by going through life continually declining opportunities to initiate behavior. They slough off the importance of getting involved in the particular activity of the moment or making contact with an available person. Their consistent refusal to reach out, or respond, becomes a gradual self-poisoning process—the poison of nonexpression. To others they may seem easygoing, unusually compatible. When it comes to a dispute about what activity to engage in, what movie to see, or what restaurant to choose, their attitude is always "It doesn't really matter to me—whatever you want is okay." Other people tend to become uncomfortable when constantly faced with this attitude. They find it hard to believe that any person can be so congenial.

The active experiencing of one's identity is largely a matter of self-expression about relatively unimportant needs and feelings as these come into the person's awareness from moment to moment. Compulsively compliant people poison themselves by their refusal to react to this inner flow of needs. Without such self-expression, they create a sort of psychic dam which holds back unbearable pressure. Their only recourse seems to be to implode (explode inwardly) as they continue to insist to the world, "It doesn't really matter."

To insist that "it really doesn't matter" is to
negate the importance of one's own existence: "I
really don't matter."

DEPRESSIONITIS

The person who suffers from depressionitis is constantly groaning about life and the miseries that always
seem to come upon him. He seems unable to go fully
into his depression and get finished with it; instead,
he keeps himself locked in by feeling sorry for himself
and clinging to his "poor little me" attitude. He refuses
to open his eyes to see if there isn't some way to
move out of his swamp of depression. He chooses to
stay with his misery.

Each of us is responsible for our own behavior in the
sense that what we do creates a pattern of reactions
which affects us in various ways, either nourishing or
toxic. When a person attempts to deny personal
responsibility for the consequences of his behavior to
himself as well as its effect on other people, he distorts
the philosophy of living *in* the moment into living *for*
the moment, and in so doing he ignores the context
(environment) in which he functions. In the most
poisonous manifestations of this pattern, the person
justifies an impulse-ridden life style in which he is
concerned only with getting his "kicks," regardless of
how destructive his behavior is to himself or others. In
its less deadly forms, the person is simply ungiving,
uncaring, unloving, and interested only in sucking
nourishment from wherever it is available. In the
world of toxic people and toxic behavior, such people
are the scavengers who only take.

CRAZYITIS

Appearing to be "crazy" can be advantageous in several ways. Various versions range from obvious manipulations to very subtle maneuvers to avoid responsibility to oneself. The victim decides to "freak out" to evade responsibility for his own actions ("I can't help it if I'm crazy").

A popular form of crazyitis is to play neurotic and undergo psychotherapy. Therapy is used as a manipulative device with which to avoid taking responsibility. The T person is not as much interested in the legitimate value of psychotherapy as he is attracted to its potential as an excuse or alibi for his irresponsibility:

> Victim to his wife who threatens to leave him: "After I get my head on straight, you'll see how loving I can be. You'll be glad you stuck it out. The doctor tells me I have deep-seated problems which make me drink or lose my temper easily. You're just like my boss—you don't understand my condition. It's easy for you to say I'm copping out; you didn't grow up with the rejections and frustration I had to put up with."

The victim poisons himself by using his hang-ups (neuroses) as an excuse. With this attitude about psychotherapy, he enters treatment in bad faith and hopes to unload responsibility for his own behavior on the therapist. He does the same kind of dumping in his relationships and subsequently feels outraged when his victim loses patience with him.

THE DUMPING SYNDROME

Some people never miss an opportunity to unload their "junk" on anyone willing to listen. The victim of this toxic pattern is caught in his own web of verbiage. He vainly hopes that if he dumps enough of his troubles on others he will free himself of them. When he is in psychotherapy, he insists that if he describes enough memories, dreams, etc. to the therapist, the therapist will find a solution to all his problems. In some cases, this person has the illusion that others enjoy, or should enjoy, his openness and desire to share.

Wives sometimes use their husbands in this way. Under the virtuous banner of "togetherness" she claims the right to dump her day's frustrations on him and feels unloved if he becomes bored, resentful or irritated with her "need to relate." She poisons herself with her helpless attitude and, in addition, drives him away. He begins to feel that his willingness to listen is like a futile attempt to fill a bottomless hole, so why bother? In marriages poisoned this way, the end result is a wife who is bitterly obsessed with her husband's withdrawal and blames her unhappiness on his indifference.

GOING OFF HALF-COCKED

Because of the possible detrimental consequences to one's well-being, it is not always realistic to take a stand against a toxic intrusion. It is healthier to tolerate a toxic pattern when the available alternatives would disrupt the person's ability to satisfy his total needs, even though they might bring relief from the poison of the immediate situation. It is a toxic effort for a person to try to resolve a poisonous situation when he doesn't have the resources to back himself up or accept the consequences of his action. It is the responsibility of each individual to take a risk to get what he wants or to avoid what he doesn't want.

Frank W. was characteristically restless and impatient. He sought desperately for ways to use up his enormous energy. At thirty-two, he was already a junior executive in a large corporation; however, he had little appreciation for his work or his achievements. He chronically complained about what he could do if only he had more authority. He had real talent and had been promised continued advancement.

A new executive joined the company who obviously felt threatened by Frank. Frank felt browbeaten and taunted by the attitude of the new executive, who was in a superior position. It was obvious to others as well as to Frank that he was being unfairly treated.

Frank decided to go directly to the president of the company with an ultimatum: "Either this guy goes or I go." Unfortunately, the president was not willing to submit to this kind of pressure, and Frank went. He had no recourse but to join a new firm and start over again in a lesser, even more boring position. He had brought the toxic intrusions of the new executive to an end, but he paid the price in other ways. He had gone off half-cocked instead of using his resources to evolve a more gradual and more effective way of solving his problem.

Toxic people tend to implement the solution that provides immediate relief without considering the consequences. If they stopped to think, they might then choose moderate alternatives that might eventually be more satisfactory.

HOLDING ON TO THE PAST

Another group of self-induced toxic behavior patterns is characterized by a person's refusal to let go of obsolete attitudes, relationships, and experiences that were part of the reality of his past, but are inappropriate in the here and now. He poisons himself with outmoded attitudes and responses which complicate his life, distracting himself from focusing on his most important needs. In the end, he loses touch with the central aspects of his self and the ongoing process of discovering his evolving identity.

THE GOOD OLD DAYS

Holding on to the past is a way of cutting oneself off from nourishment in the present. Some people constantly complain about their present problems, and about social conditions, world affairs, etc., as if everything were bleak and nothing good ever happened. They contrast this with the "good old days" when people were more friendly and cared about one another. While there may be some minimal gratification in reminiscing about what living was like many years ago, the toxic effect can be quite devastating.

Memory is notoriously inaccurate; the past is a collection of fantasies. When a person clings to these fantasies and insists that his past really was as glorious as he remembers, he convinces himself that the present is dull, drab, and depressing. This kind of self-poisoning attitude destroys the nourishment (excitement, joy, and pleasure) in what *is*.

Mr. Brown to his family on the Fourth of July: "Those fireworks weren't bad, but they just don't make 'em like they used to. When I was a kid, firecrackers had a much bigger bang and there were lots more of them. We really had fun in those days!"

BOXED-IN-ITIS

FEMALE PATIENT: I'm convinced that men just won't like me when they get to know me. When they see what's really inside me, they'll run away. I just don't have much to offer, and sooner or later, they'll find that out.

THERAPIST: You've already told me of several lengthy relationships you've had, including a marriage which lasted ten years. Surely some of these men knew what you were really like.

PATIENT: Yes, but those men weren't very discriminating. They would accept almost anybody. They were really all slobs, and any woman could make them happy.

When a person decides to cling to a self-poisoning attitude, he will always find reasons, explanations, and excuses to justify his attitude. In this way, people box themselves in with variations on the theme "My mind is made up; don't confuse me with reality."

They seem to insist on rigidly maintaining a self-poisoning attitude in the face of experiences and relationships that are contrary to their fixed position; they become deaf, dumb, and blind. They refuse to see the contradictory data of their own experiences, even when this could provide them with greater nourishment. Boxing oneself in with fixed ways of relating, or life style, provides the comfort and security of the old and familiar. To step out of one's box and explore new possibilities for more gratifying ways of being also brings with it the fear and anxiety of the unknown. Some people throughout their entire lives choose poison over uncertainty.

REBELLIONITIS

Toxic people exhaust themselves with their fantasies of oppression. For example, the "pseudo hippie," lacking any real interest in nourishing himself or confronting his own hang-ups, becomes a rebel for the sake of being a rebel—it's better than being nothing. In the process, he latches on to movements or joins groups to which he never feels honestly committed. His phony rebellion ironically emerges as a "way out" brand of conformity. This pattern is also observable in some members of extreme political groups, liberal or reactionary, and in various fanatical religious sects. They rebel automatically and compulsively against everything that fails to support their dogma. Their rebellion does not reflect their personal convictions and integrity; rather, it is an elaborately disguised scheme to escape the self. As a result, they realize little nourishment for the enormous energy they invest. The self-deprivation of this T pattern is reflected in the increasing rigidity and desperation of their efforts; the more they starve themselves, the more they redouble the intensity of their efforts. The end result is fanaticism, which in itself reflects the psychological death of the victim's identity.

THE AVENGER

Most people feel at times that they have been abused, neglected, and treated unfairly or even cruelly. The avenger invests enormous amounts of his energy seeking vengeance in one way or another. In this activity's poisonous form, the avenger simply enjoys hurting other people, as if to lessen the pain he himself has experienced. Sometimes he chooses a career that can serve as an outlet for his vengeance. When he does his job well, someone else suffers in some way or is "brought to justice." Or, the avenger may dwell on the misery of others as he futilely seeks satisfaction (nourishment) from other people's misfortunes. He poisons himself further by a refusal to let go of past grievances. Any satisfaction he may receive is temporary, and ultimately the avenger is left empty again.

"I'LL OUTLAST YOU"

This is a frequent pattern in toxic marriages in which one or both partners are committed to a war to the finish. Having decided, for various reasons, that they can't (i.e., won't) dissolve the marriage, they engage in an ongoing campaign in which each seems interested in deliberately irritating the other. Their pattern is one of mutual frustration and vindictiveness.

While the toxic interaction is obvious, the endless battle to which each partner commits himself is also a virulent self-poisoning process. The winner also loses. The one who may succeed in literally burying the other has paid an enormous price in the neglect of his own nourishment and growth.

CONCLUSION

Emotional nourishment depends on our willingness to take responsibility for the ongoing process of being aware how we nourish and poison ourself. The concepts of self-generated nourishment and toxicity reflect an orientation toward life as a whole. Each of us makes our choice. We can poison ourselves by neglecting our own needs, or we can commit ourselves to the process of discovering how to become a more effective self-nourisher. Each of us must accept the fact that we cannot avoid making such choices and that we will inevitably experience the consequences of our choices. When our choices are too inconsistent with our basic needs, we become fragmented and stagnate our own growth. Fragmenting activities are "dis-integrating" to the whole person.

The many kinds of self-induced poisons are all forms of self-destruction: the person in various ways chooses to tear himself apart. Explanations of *why* a person is poisoning himself only serve as excuses for not living in the here and now. Every day of our lives, each of us must make the choice between nourishment and poison.

CHAPTER FOUR

Self-induced Loneliness

Frequently a person is only vaguely aware of how he experiences being alone. When his aloneness has the nourishing quality of solitude, he often deprives himself of the full nourishment of this experience by his lack of awareness. When his prevalent experience in being alone is loneliness, a lack of awareness handicaps his ability to seek antidotes for his loneliness. The following comparative attitudes and behavior patterns may clarify the reader's awareness of when his aloneness is nourishing (solitude) or toxic (loneliness).

1. **Solitude:** Do I look forward to brief periods of time (several hours) when I know I will be alone with feelings of eagerness and excitement?

   or

   Loneliness: Do I begin to feel anxious and worry about how I will "kill the time" that I will be spending alone?

2. **Solitude:** Do I sometimes feel "peopled out" and long to be by myself?

   or

Loneliness: Do I "never get enough of people" and see very little point in being by myself?

3. **Solitude:** Do I enjoy certain private experiences and at times find myself not wanting to share these with others?

or

Loneliness: Do I feel that nothing is as good if you experience it alone?

4. **Solitude:** Do I have to choose between various pleasures which I enjoy alone because I lack the time for all of them?

or

Loneliness: Do I find myself making an effort to plan activities to occupy my time and feel anxious that I might become bored?

5. **Solitude:** Do I like being only with me, and enjoy myself?

or

Loneliness: Am I easily bored with myself and generally feel as if there is little within me that is exciting or stimulating?

6. **Solitude:** When someone wants to spend time with me, am I aware that when I choose to be with that person I *give up* being just with myself?

or

Loneliness: Do I always feel I will enjoy myself more if I am with someone else than if I am alone?

7. **Solitude:** Do I sometimes seek solitude even away from those I live with and love?

or

Loneliness: Do I always want their company

even if I am doing something by myself (reading, watching television)?

8. **Solitude:** Am I *primarily* centered on myself and the meaning I experience for myself in my life style?

or

Loneliness: Am I primarily oriented toward how others experience activities, so that the meaning of my experience depends *primarily* on the reactions of others?

9. **Solitude:** Are my excitement and joy *primarily* based on my own experiencing of the moment, whether alone or with someone else?

or

Loneliness: Are my excitement and joy essentially triggered by the reaction of others around me?

10. **Solitude:** Are many of my interests focused on experiences that do not involve relating to others?

or

Loneliness: Does practically everything I do that I experience as meaningful involve my relationships with other people?

11. **Solitude:** Am I aware of having ended some relationships because I would rather be by myself than with that particular person?

or

Loneliness: Do I generally feel that a person "can never have too many friends" and give up my time alone rather than risk alienating anyone?

12. **Solitude:** When I feel lonely, am I able to tolerate my loneliness without excessive anxiety?

or

Loneliness: When I feel lonely, do I easily become anxious or panicky?

13. **Solitude:** Can I accept occasional rejection from someone I care about deeply without feeling abandoned and isolated?

or

Loneliness: Does rejection send me into an emotional upheaval that is difficult to tolerate?

14. **Solitude:** Am I comfortable telling others when I want solitude and when I feel lonely and need contact?

or

Loneliness: Am I afraid to tell others I want to be by myself and embarrassed to admit when I feel lonely?

15. **Solitude:** Do I experience my time alone as something I want to enjoy with full awareness?

or

Loneliness: Do I anesthetize myself with alcohol or drugs when alone?

The emotional distress from loneliness is reaching epidemic proportions in today's world and is a major reason growing numbers of people experience their lives as a struggle lacking in purpose. These people feel increasingly cut off from themselves (fragmented), from others (alienated), and from nature and the universe of which they are a part.

Loneliness is a feeling of deprivation of emotionally satisfying relationships. It is a self-induced toxic state of psychic withdrawal and psychic isolation. Knowingly or not, the lonely person activates and sustains behavior patterns with which he produces his loneliness. Regardless of the type of attitudes and behavior

patterns, lonely people experience the same consequence: when they interact with others, the end product is predominantly rejection (theirs or the other
person's), lack of emotional involvement, emotional
deprivation, and frustration.

Feelings of loneliness are probably experienced by
everyone. A person may feel lonely even during a brief
period when he is out of touch with others. The lonely
person tends to experience himself, his world, and
other people as lacking in interest and excitement. He
has a more limited attention span and quickly becomes
bored and restless when sufficient external stimulation
is not forthcoming.

A person who feels dedicated to some kind of life-
work may choose largely to ignore his need for intimacy in favor of what he feels are more important
needs and may not feel lonely or frustrated. For the
person whose existence is a struggle for physical survival, intimacy may be a minor need and feelings of
loneliness extremely rare or nonexistent.

Loneliness becomes more of a problem in cultures
where the normal demands of survival and basic physical needs are generally satisfied. A person's existence
is then increasingly focused on gratification of his emotional needs. The lonely person may be quite successful in various aspects of living; but often he has failed
to learn to relate to others in meaningful and intimate
ways.

At age thirty-three, Roger began to wonder
whether someone had put a hex on him. He had
many enduring relationships with friends of both
sexes, yet somehow had never been able to sustain an intimate relationship with a woman. Unbe-

lievably, over the years, he had gone steady with nine different women, six of whom subsequently married old boy friends. The rest terminated their relationships with him, each expressing her desire to remain "good friends." Not once had he instigated the breakup. Not once had the breakup been a consequence of a fight or quarrel. Roger was a nice-looking, pleasant, easygoing guy who everyone agreed would make a great father and family man. He simply didn't know how to relate intimately. His behavior was full of superficial interactions. He was always available for a poker game, to go bowling, or as an extra man at a party. Roger desperately felt his loneliness and was confused and baffled by his continual rejection by women. All he ever heard when he asked for an explanation was a response to the effect that "You're a nice guy, but you just don't turn me on." He didn't know how to behave any differently.

The lonely person usually is so caught up with his own self that he pays little attention to how others experience him.

Some people are continuously involved in meaningful relationships, while others live in constant crisis over their need for intimacy. They may never establish enduring feelings of belonging. If they do, they still worry that they may be lonely in the future. Others follow a cyclical pattern in which they have frequent transitory relationships, with intervening gaps of loneliness. Loneliness and the fear of loneliness may dominate a person's life.

To avoid the dread of loneliness, some people enter into and remain in poisonous relationships. Some marry to escape loneliness, then live in anguish rather than face the isolated existence they anticipate with divorce. Others drive themselves toward achievement and success, even choose their career in the hope that it will insure them against loneliness. Parents often cling to their children for the same reason.

The lonely person is responsible for his loneliness. *How* does he actively go about making himself lonely? How does he go about preserving and intensifying his loneliness? He may know exactly how he does it. More frequently, however, he is unaware of how he drives others away or makes himself unapproachable or unavailable for nourishing interaction.

LONELINESS AND SOLITUDE

Loneliness and solitude are directly opposite kinds of experiences in being alone. Aloneness includes any state of psychic isolation from others, ranging from intolerable loneliness and a desperate need for human contact to enormously gratifying states of solitude in which the presence of another is unwelcome or even intrusive.

In solitude, there is no feeling of deprivation from the lack of contact with others. The person does not feel the need to interact. He is engrossed with his inner feelings and experiences. Behaviorally, he is introverted; emotionally, he is in touch with himself and what he is experiencing. Solitude is a gratifying and enriching experience. Solitude can be an exciting experience of exhilaration, with intense feelings of aliveness.

Loneliness does not necessarily derive from the physical absence of other people. Some who live isolated lives feel deprivation and pain while others living in similar isolation do not. Conversely, some people have an abundance of human interaction and are quite lonely. They may feel intensely dissatisfied yet remain unaware that their frustration is the pain of their loneliness. For the most part, lonely people are aware that they are lonely but refuse to accept responsibility for it, preferring to blame circumstances, bad luck, etc. Others feel that there is nothing more they can do, they have tried everything, and they are destined to be lonely.

The lonely person poisons himself by behavior patterns that cut him off from others and leave him emotionally isolated. Poisonous behavior is more often the cause rather than the result of loneliness. The essential truth is that these poisonous behavior patterns are responsible for sustaining a lonely person's loneliness.

The lonely person tries to manipulate others into taking responsibility for his needs. He is often full of demands and expectations of others, while maintaining his own role of helplessness and futility. An honest interest in being nourishing to others is frequently the farthest thing from his mind. Each lonely person rejects people in his own way and according to his own particular pattern of instigating and sustaining his isolating self-poisonous behavior.

Healthy, aware individuals seek relationships with other nourishing people. The lonely person is usually left with other toxic people who are also lonely. These people may appear to escape their loneliness with each other; however, by holding on to these relationships, they are less available for new, potentially more nourishing ones.

It often appears that the emotional distress of loneliness happens to a person against his will. No one would choose loneliness, any more than he would choose to have a dread disease. Often lonely people go to considerable effort to alleviate their loneliness. As the pain increases and the hunger for intimacy mounts, the lonely person may initiate a frenzy of activities in an effort to end his unwanted isolation. Such efforts are apt to be ineffective, since they ignore the behavior patterns that create his loneliness. Redoubling such attempts only increases his frustration and desperation as his emotional alienation continues.

When a person feels too threatened by intimacy with others, he may choose isolation as the lesser of two evils. This choice does effectively protect him from his dreaded fear of rejection. Some kind of loneliness-producing pattern then becomes a significant aspect of his life style. The woman who is constantly the innocent victim of one unhappy romance after another may be reacting to her fear of deep involvement and subsequent rejection. For example, in order to protect herself from intimacy, knowingly or not, she may continually involve herself with men who are unsuitable for enduring, intimate relationships.

By the time Mary was thirty-four, she had been married and divorced three times. Each of her husbands was an alcoholic. At the time they met, each had given up drinking for at least six months and in one instance four years. Her father had died of a liver ailment directly attributed to excessive drinking. She herself did not drink at all. At the age of ten she had already resolved never to date anyone who drank.

With each of her husbands, she sincerely believed that his drinking problem was past and would not recur. While seemingly she sought a nourishing relationship, there was from the beginning a built-in insurance policy against a lasting relationship. After marriage, each husband began drinking again within a relatively short time. This evoked a violent reaction from her, and the relationship rapidly deteriorated.

It is rare to find a lonely person who does not have an intense fear of rejection. In this case, Mary enjoyed the comfortable feeling of the familiar that she experienced with men who had had a drinking problem. She was unaware of her immediate responsiveness to them: "Somehow, I just feel more at ease when I meet a man who has been an alcoholic." T people often experience a feeling of safety in relating to others who show familiar behavior patterns even though these are the same patterns that have been so poisonous to them in the past.

Frequently, a lonely person is aware of his general unhappiness, which he experiences as tension, anxiety, or restlessness, although often he is unaware of the specific meaning of these symptom messages and may not know what he should do to alleviate his discontent. Loneliness is often masked by façades of "busywork," obsessive preoccupation with success, achievement of end goals, the use of drugs and alcohol, etc. Such façades blind the person's awareness of what he really needs.

When hidden loneliness persists, a person attempts

to counter his mounting frustration by pursuing even more intensely whatever forms of escape he has developed. The lonely businessman, as his emotional deprivation increases, intensifies his activities and becomes obsessed with business. The frustrated housewife increasingly turns to her tranquilizers to dull the pain of her boredom and loneliness. Without awareness, a person has little choice but to pursue any ways he has found that provide some relief, however brief and ineffective.

LONELINESS-INDUCING GAMES

The descriptive patterns that follow illustrate some of the ways people create their loneliness. These games not only create loneliness; they also produce other toxic reactions to the person himself and to others.

SOMEBODY FILL ME UP

The lonely person often feels unable to initiate any effective solution to his emptiness and passively looks to the world to hand him what he needs. His helpless attitude places the burden on others. His cry is "Here I am! Somebody please love me! I need it desperately!" The nourishing person will back away from this kind of relating because of the insatiable demands being imposed. The lonely person rarely is aware of this toxic attitude and continues to experience his loneliness as a mystifying puzzle.

June could be described only as a self-adoring person who expected the world to do her bidding. She was a beautiful child and clearly her parents' favorite. She had four older brothers, and her arrival was the fulfillment of a dream for both her father ("I always wanted a little girl I could spoil rotten") and her mother ("Now I can share things with her I never had when I was growing up"). Her four brothers had been repeatedly admonished by both parents to "take care of little sister." She was voted the most popular girl in school, was chosen prom queen in her senior year, and had been considered by a talent scout for a movie contract. Her exceptional beauty only enhanced her expectation that the world would be happy to do her bidding. During her college years and later, men clamored to win her favor. Her husband too adored her and took constant delight in pleasing her with gifts, exotic vacations, and other surprises.

June had continuously postponed having children, offering a variety of excuses to her husband, who wanted a large family. Their marriage reached a crisis when, at thirty-three, she still wanted to postpone having a family. Her husband's patience was at an end, and he decided to leave, assuring her that he would come back when she was ready to have children. He never returned home, and she never asked him to. A year later he asked her for a divorce, informing her that he had met someone else. June was outraged, as were her parents, at his "lack of consideration."

Her parents, of course, were quick to assure her that she would find another husband who would really appreciate her. Various men did show a genuine interest in her. However, when they did not respond with the adoration and solicitude she had come to expect, she became indignant and would stop seeing them. She continued this dating pattern for several years, becoming aware of an increasing loneliness which the love and admiration of her family no longer alleviated. She was honestly baffled that men were not delighted to do her bidding for the sheer joy of winning her favor. She concluded, quite erroneously, that they were simply interested in her sexually and decided that she would "wait until the right one comes along."

She moved in with her parents shortly after her divorce. Gradually she stopped dating and became increasingly withdrawn and irritable, particularly toward her parents, whose continuing solicitude seemed to be increasingly frustrating to her. She honestly had no awareness of how she had alienated herself and created her lonely existence.

Often the lonely person proclaims to the world that he has "a lot to give" if only he could find the right person to appreciate him. Intimacy is an attitude and a way of being; it is not some kind of prize package one can hope to find or to work hard enough to deserve. The lonely person's attitude of withholding his love is often a façade with which he deceives himself. Actually, he is constantly evaluating others like a personnel manager screening people for a job. The "job" goes unfilled and the person remains lonely— *and* safe from his fear of intimacy and his dread of choosing the "wrong" person.

This pattern occurs in some unusually attractive

women who have many relationships with men and yet remain unmarried, and in men who fear that all women are "just looking for security." In each instance, no one meets their expectations, so that they continue to remain isolated (and safe-guarded) from intimate relating.

HOLIER THAN THOU

This brand of self-induced loneliness is popular among the "psychologically sophisticated." The message they send to others is "If you have hang-ups, you're not for me," or "Get yourself straightened out first, and then we'll see." The implication of holier-than-thou people is "I have hang-ups too [thus demonstrating their liberal, enlightened attitudes], but they are minor, especially in the light of my far greater assets. If you have any real hang-ups, you are automatically ineligible for an intimate relationship with me."

Lonely people tend to be excessively critical, which is an opposite attitude to intimate relating.

LOSER-ORIENTED PATTERNS

Picking "losers" means selecting people who cannot really satisfy what the person knows he wants in a relationship. Loneliness is often sustained by the person's continually selecting "losers" and investing his time and energy in them. For some men, the last woman they will approach is exactly the one they

would most like to meet. Instead, they select those
women who present less of a challenge. Attractive
women sometimes complain that many interesting
men seem afraid to approach them. Instead, such
men choose to become involved with women they find
less exciting and less interesting but who are also less
threatening.

Single women who repeatedly involve themselves
with married men insure themselves against long-last-
ing relationships and increase the likelihood of per-
petual loneliness. They use a variety of rationalizations
to justify beginning a relationship with a man who is
obviously unavailable ("I'll keep it light"; "Why not?";
"I know just where I stand"). They avoid their
anxiety and suffer the loneliness of a sporadic, unstable relationship. In all likelihood, despite the woman's
best intentions, she becomes increasingly emotionally
involved, while continuing to live on the fringes of his
life. As time passes, she becomes emotionally unavailable to other men. They bore her; they are uninteresting; she keeps thinking of her lover. This may continue
for years until eventually there is a breakup which is
apt to be unusually devastating. The woman experiences the despair and loss of a love relationship without ever having had the intimacy of a mutually sharing
full relationship.

WHAT IF PEOPLE KNEW

Self-induced loneliness may be deliberately initiated
by the person who is convinced that if others really
knew him they would have nothing to do with him.
He hides what he considers to be unacceptable in himself, although frequently he doesn't even know what

this is. On this basis, he is convinced that he is unlovable and unacceptable. To the degree to which he remains too fearful to risk expressing himself, he remains fragmented and isolated from full intimacy with others.

Men in particular often consider their "weaknesses" to be so intolerable that they must be forever hidden. Particularly in the presence of others, but even in solitude, they totally reject their need to cry. They may consider any fear to be a fault that would disillusion others about their manliness. They believe that to express emotions, particularly anxieties, constitutes failure as a man and must be avoided at all costs. The effect, of course, is to create barriers even against the women they love, marry, and live with. Since such men never reveal their true responses, the degree of possible intimacy in any relationship is permanently limited.

Other forms of "unacceptable impulses" with which a person may isolate himself include fantasies that he is strange, perverted, or "crazy." These fantasies maintain their power to destroy primarily by remaining hidden. The person is convinced that he would be labeled weird, perverted, or insane. He chooses to go through life fragmenting his self unnecessarily and sustaining his barrier against deeper intimacy.

Breaking a pattern of loneliness may mean gradually revealing the "unacceptable parts" of oneself in an intimate relationship. Only in this way can a person know whether the other will really accept him as he is.

Culturally unacceptable impulses include feelings and actions that in childhood were loaded with guilt and shame and therefore represent whole areas of the person that are unacceptable and must be hidden.

Stanley grew up in a home in which his parents were constantly fighting and arguing. While their fights never led to physical violence, his father repeatedly threatened physical attack and would at times pound his fists vehemently against a table or wall. His mother's characteristic response was "You might just as well hit me; you're killing me anyway." When these arguments were particularly intense, Stanley would become frightened to the point of panic. He was aware of vague feelings that, somehow, it was his fault that his parents argued so much. As far back as he could remember, he had become frightened when anyone got angry. On rare occasions, he would become irritable or upset about something. His mother's reaction of "You're turning out just like your father" terrorized him, and he would literally beg his mother's forgiveness.

By the time Stanley entered high school, he needed to act out a ritual with his mother in which he would insist that she tell him exactly three times that she had no anger toward him and that she loved him. When his mother balked at doing this or called it nonsense, he would become so anxious that she eventually went along with his obsessive need for absolution. His father would accuse his mother of ruining their son—"Look what you've done: he's afraid to open his mouth." This would frequently result in another fight,

which only added to Stanley's already intolerable
guilt feelings.

In his junior year in high school, the counselor
recommended family therapy. This helped to
alleviate the friction in the home, and Stanley
seemed to settle down to a more stable adjustment. He became a quiet, introverted man with
a very passive, withdrawn life style. He dated
infrequently throughout his twenties and early
thirties. He related to people by passively comply-
ing with what they wanted, while continuing to
suppress the growing pressure of his unexpressed
anger. He never broke off a relationship (he was
absolutely unwilling to be angry or to reject anyone), but became increasingly noncommunicative.
When he wanted to end a relationship, he would
become so malleable and compliant that the
woman would eventually become exasperated
and break off with him.

Stanley had a job with a large accounting firm,
where he was an exemplary employee. As he grew
older, he refused more and more social invitations.
His increasing withdrawal reflected his overwhelming fear: "I would rather continue to suffer
my longing for intimate involvement than risk
anyone's getting angry at me, or take the chance
that anyone might see my anger and resentments."

As a child, he had learned that his resentment
toward his parents was totally unacceptable. Such
impulses continued to dominate him in adult life,
and he continued to see them as intolerable parts
of himself which would cause him to be shunned
by everyone—if people ever found out.

THE "BEING HURT" FANTASY

Loneliness can be self-induced by a belief that if one is rebuffed, the pain will be catastrophic. In response to this fear, many lonely people have insulated themselves emotionally by building psychic barriers to prevent anyone from getting close to them. Their fear of rejection is such that they greatly exaggerate the pain of being rejected. In essence, they are phobic about life and choose the protection of casual, superficial relationships. When they feel growing intimacy with another person, they invariably end the relationship. In the most obvious sense, they choose their loneliness.

THE STORM TROOPER

Some lonely people are puzzled by their lack of intimacy because they feel they have a genuine interest in others. They consider themselves extraverted, and indeed they are. Their "fascination" with others may take the form of intense, wide-eyed attention to the other person's every comment and a barrage of questions, which the victim is likely to experience as an invasion rather than an inviting gesture toward contact. Or the "blitzkrieg" comes in the form of a heated argument which the storm trooper insists is only a "stimulating discussion." Sometimes, after listening closely to show how interested he is, he decides to "share himself" and then proceeds to monopolize the conversation, oblivious to the boredom of his listener. He is unable to perceive others as individuals, much less appreciate them as people. Instead, his preoccupation is with doing his thing, and he leaves little or no room for the needs of other people for self-expression.

Relating to another on an intimate level means really listening with all one's senses. Only in this way can one know the other person as he is.

PSYCHIC ANESTHESIA

The use of alcohol and drugs is frequently an effective way of inducing psychic isolation. Many people drink or use tranquilizers and other drugs to be more open and outgoing, and superficially this goal is accomplished; conversation flows more easily, tension is reduced, and the person may be more able to enjoy himself. However, anesthetizing one's inhibitions does not lessen the underlying withdrawal pattern. Rather, the opposite occurs, since avoidance of anxiety and fear increases their threatening quality. In addition, the person's potential for learning to cope more effectively with his fears is also anesthetized. The effect is usually a psychological dependency on alcohol or drugs in social settings. Over a period of time, the person's openness without his artificial "relating aids" diminishes while his withdrawal tendencies increase.

It is paradoxical that the more successful a person is in concealing his anxiety, the more empty he is apt to feel inside. Over a period of years people become very skillful at concealing characteristics that they feel are unacceptable. Yet inwardly they are tormented with feelings of inadequacy and self-contempt. Because their inner pain is so intense, it is difficult for them to believe that it does not show. Conversely, the more aware they become of how effectively they have fooled others, the more they come to believe that they would be rejected were they to drop their pretenses.

> Only when a person allows another to experience his spontaneous self is it possible for him to believe that the other person is really able to respond with love, appreciation, and caring.

THE JOKER

The joker must be the life of the party at all times. He must be clever, amusing, and witty whenever others are present. He is also a subtle saboteur. Serious or intimate conversations sometimes do occur, but they are apt to be short-lived. At the point at which the other person may feel some real closeness, he is undercut by the joker's ubiquitous humor, which wipes out the previous intimacy. Inappropriate joking and laughter can be extremely poisonous to the growing depth of a relationship. The joker's acquaintances—and that's the extent of his relationships—learn never to take him seriously, and they count on him for only one thing: a lot of laughs. Frequently, the joker himself is the victim of deep depression and loneliness—about which he will also try to joke.

SEXUALITY AS AN AVOIDANCE OF INTIMACY

The acceptance of sex education and the availability of material on sex techniques is a two-edged sword. Knowledge about sex can enhance the intimacy between two people. It can also become an end in itself that short-circuits the growth of deeper feelings, and this is how the lonely person often uses his own sexuality. A man may use sex largely to display his talents and impress his partner. It is not infrequent that this is his primary gratification in the sex act. In a nourishing relationship, sex is an expression of emotional union and intimate sharing. For the "sex technician," sex is essentially manipulation, an end in itself, and rarely evolves into deeper feelings of love. This is the pattern of many young adults, heterosexual or homosexual, who find themselves confronted with increasing loneliness and feelings of emptiness despite constant sexual activity.

Sexual promiscuity is a not-so-subtle way of avoiding intimate relationships. "One-nighters" of both sexes are willing to engage in physical intimacy as long as they feel no threat of becoming emotionally involved. Promiscuous people are usually lonely. While sometimes promiscuity is an expression of desperate longing for contact, it nevertheless tends to prevent one from finding longer-lasting relationships.

WELL, WHY NOT

Lonely people often refuse to be discriminating even when they are aware that a particular relationship is poisonous to them. A woman may date a man she doesn't particularly enjoy only because he takes her out. She refuses to consider that this makes her less available for a more meaningful relationship while she is settling for minor gratifications. A man may date a woman purely for sex and feel he is outmaneuvering her by getting her into bed without making any commitment himself. Such patterns of manipulation lead to countermanipulations and only create the emptiness and frustration of pseudo intimacy. Any pattern in which a person settles solely for secondary gratifications is a detour away from nourishment and toward loneliness.

ALONENESS PHOBIA

For some lonely people there is no such thing as pleasurable solitude. The need of such a person to avoid being alone is often compulsive. He may have schedules of activities to fill any void, even a single evening, and a priority list of people he can call should some free time occur. He may even keep track of exactly how many names he has and fanatically maintain his list at a reassuring number. What is important to him is the quantity of contacts, rather than caring for those people or appreciating their individuality or uniqueness. He fills his time but perpetuates his loneliness, since he is interested in others as a means to an end. Because he is so preoccupied with escaping loneliness, he does not have time to form real relationships.

His list of casual friends usually consists of others who are also lonely and readily available. They too have developed toxic ways of relating and have little nourishment to give. Their mutual emptiness is often revealed in their expectant expressions when a new member enters their group; perhaps he can provide some healthy excitement. Their disappointments are continual and inevitable, yet they persist in sustaining their "contacts" and schedules in order to avoid being alone.

It rarely occurs to lonely people to take the risks of reaching out *in spite of* their anxiety and fearfulness to others who might offer more nourishing relationships.

HOW COULD YOU DO THIS TO ME?

Some chronically lonely people insist that they are willing to go "more than halfway" with others. At the same time, they complain that somehow they have been undeservedly abused and manipulated. They project their self-induced loneliness onto the rest of the world. They insist that their expectations are reasonable—even meager.

For example, the domineering mother who cries to her child that "All I want is for you to be happy!" really means "All I want is to make the major decisions in your life." When, in adulthood, the child finally takes his stand and refuses to be poisoned further, the bewildered mother cannot believe "that my own child would desert me after all I've done for him."

Once a relationship is established on the basis of pressure or entrapment (*e.g.*, inducing feelings of guilt), the lonely person dares not let go of his manipulative games. Usually he senses that his manipulations have usurped the freedom of the other person to relate as *he* chooses. Manipulation always suffocates intimacy.

WALLS OF AVOIDANCE

An experienced waiter can walk the length of a restaurant without catching the eye of a single customer. Similarly, the lonely person feeds his loneliness by avoiding contact. His eyes are usually looking either

down or away, and he seldom looks at anyone for
more than an instant—least of all if the other person
should look back. He rarely smiles and often has a
stony expression that makes him difficult to approach.
In this way he may have developed such an effective
mask of self-containment that in actuality his life is
largely limited to his inner world.

Going about looking as if one were totally self-
reliant and independent and didn't need anything from anyone is a façade hiding a deep
longing for intimacy.

Making contact with such a person requires unusual
persistence and tenacity. It is possible that an aware
person can develop a relationship with someone who
seems aloof. However, those who hide themselves
increase the odds against getting what they want in
this world. Instead, they tend to ensure that they will
remain lonely.

BEING PRESENT IN BODY ONLY

Talking to a person who is uninterested in contact
is like talking to a well-trained yes-man. His attention
floats everywhere as he shows only sporadic interest
in anyone while inwardly daydreaming, fantasizing,
or thinking about other things. His responses are polite,
but indicate his lack of attention. Since he's not really
there, no nourishment emanates from him, nor is he
available to receive any. In relating, he leaves the
other person hanging in a frustrated, unfinished situa-

tion. Typically, the other person senses that he is not really interested. N people will abandon this fruitless process in short order and leave the person to himself. Those who usually seem detached and uninterested in other people bring their loneliness on themselves by their constant avoidance. Being blinded and out of contact, they fail to "see" others who are available and interested.

BUSYWORK

This popular brand of self-induced loneliness is subtle, since the person's overt behavior appears to be the opposite of a withdrawing, isolating pattern.

Jeffrey remembered his childhood as having been lonely. He grew up in an exclusive suburb in the hills overlooking a large metropolitan area. He rarely saw other children in his neighborhood, since the winding streets were dangerous for play, and there were no sidewalks. The remoteness of his home made it even more difficult to find playmates his own age. Even the maid had to be picked up by car from the nearest bus line, three miles away. His brother was six years older and had always been totally uninterested in Jeffrey. He considered his sister, who was only two years younger, a nuisance or, at best, someone to tease. He was starved for human contact. "Both my parents always seemed to be away or rushing around doing one thing or another. I felt that when they did pay attention to me, it was mainly because they didn't want to hurt my feelings. I knew they loved me, but I didn't feel they understood what I needed."

Jeffrey graduated from medical school with top honors and rapidly gained a reputation as an outstanding cardiovascular surgeon. In addition to his busy practice, he participated in medical-association activities and made frequent lecture tours. He often flew to various parts of the country when called in as a consultant by his medical colleagues. For years he had instructed his wife to keep a suitcase packed and ready at all times for such emergency trips.

Jeffrey was perplexed by recurring periods of depression which seemed to increase over the years. "This is absolutely absurd. I know this is some functional [psychological] disorder. I'm increasingly irritated with these moods of mine, which really distract me from my work" was his statement to the therapist in his initial consultation. Jeffrey's wife was also very active and seemed to flourish on social activities and organizational work. She too suffered from these periodic depressions. Her solution was constant use of tranquilizers. Obviously, the family life was remarkably similar to that in which Jeffrey grew up. They too lived in a remote suburb, with their two daughters.

Jeffrey's first severe depression occurred when his second daughter left home for college. "They grew up so fast! I never really got to know them!" His self-prescribed solution for his depression was more activity, and he accepted a faculty position at a local medical school in addition to his other activities. His colleagues sometimes kidded him about being "the busiest doctor in town" and jokingly warned him that he might not be immune to cardiovascular disease himself. His response was always "I flourish on work. I don't know what I would do without it."

He was totally unaware of exactly how true his statement was. His day-to-day activities were dictated by his appointment book. When he and his wife were alone, they found they had long since forgotten how to simply enjoy each other and share any intimate relating. Their sex life was perfunctory and their dialogues superficial and focused on events and happenings. Each night his wife took her sleeping pills and went to bed. It was then that Jeffrey felt the gnawing feeling in his stomach most intensely. (He had no idea that it was loneliness gnawing at him.) His life was meaningful primarily because of his professional activities, through which he could escape his loneliness.

When he suffered a mild coronary, his whole life style crumbled. He knew he could survive and live a normal life, but only if he were willing to cut his strenuous schedule drastically. This he did—only to find that his leisure time now created a new stress. He didn't know what to do with himself and began to show signs of irritability, restlessness, and emotional strain. He developed what was diagnosed as a "severe anxiety neurosis with strong depressive features."

Reluctantly, Jeffrey began intensive psychotherapy. He initially flew into a rage when the therapist suggested that he was essentially a very lonely man. His rage melted into a flood of tears (the first time he had cried since he was a small boy). He then verbalized the fleeting awareness that he had had, over the years, of feeling lonely and frightened. He suddenly realized that he had buried these feelings in a frenzy of activities.

Antidotes to loneliness often begin with the difficult task of confronting ourselves with the urgent need for meaningful relationships.

THE EMBARRASSMENT OF LONELINESS

For some people, the most painful part of their loneliness is the shame of other people's knowing about it. Their main effort, then, is not to discover ways of overcoming the real problem, but to create a façade of "happiness and belongingness" that will successfully hide the truth from others. Such people may radiate an air of indifference, snobbishness, or aloofness as if to emphasize that they don't need anyone. As they learn to play this deceptive game more skillfully, their mask tends to guarantee their isolation. They succeed only in avoiding the embarrassment of being "caught" in their loneliness, which, they believe, would be far worse than the loneliness itself.

> *In a joint consultation, the following dialogue took place between LaVerne, a thirty-six-year-old divorcée with no children, and Harry, who was forty-two, had been divorced for three years, and had two children. They had gone together for more than a year, and Harry wanted to marry her. She had consistently rejected marriage, at the same time acknowledging that she cared for him.*

The appointment with the therapist was made by Harry, who was increasingly angry at LaVerne's refusal to make a commitment. His growing irritation was beginning to disrupt their relationship.

HARRY: I just don't understand why you don't want to get married.

LAVERNE: That's an old-fashioned sentimental trip. Who needs it?

HARRY: I thought you loved me. You certainly said it enough times when we were close or making love.

LAVERNE: That's a dirty trick. You catch me when I'm off guard and then throw it back in my face that I said I loved you.

H: Well, if you don't love me, I'd like you to tell me.

L: *(Her face reddening in obvious embarrassment)* Well, uh—uh—not in front of the doctor . . . Harry, I care for you—you know that . . .

H: This is how you frustrate me. Just tell me whether you love me or not. If you don't, I'll go away. I won't bother you any more.

L: You're crowding me. I'm happy the way things are. I don't want to get trapped into marriage.

H: Seeing you a couple of times a week and knowing you're dating other men is too hard for me. I miss you and feel lonely even when I try to date other women. It's you I want to be with. Don't you ever feel lonely?

L: *(Now really blushing, one foot wiggling up and down)* Jesus, Harry, you ask such dumb questions. What's this lonely business? *(Sounding contemptuous)* Me, lonely . . . that's silly. I've got people calling me all the time. *(Obviously*

angry) How could you even ask such a dumb
question?

H: You see what I'm up against, Doctor. We've had
this argument many times. Yet when I start to
walk out, she stops me and tells me not to go—
that she needs me.

L: Dammit, Harry, you're embarrassing me.

H: Well, it's true, isn't it?

L: *(Now very frustrated)* You really embarrass me.
What do you want me to do, crawl to you?

H: *(Quite surprised)* Now, *that's* really weird. I
asked you if you love me and you say I'm asking
you to crawl to me. I guess there's no hope for
us. I guess you are happy with all your friends.
You don't need me. I'm the one who needs a
more intimate relationship.

L: Sometimes I think you're a sentimental fool,
Harry. You're too old-fashioned.

Finally, several weeks later, Harry gave up and
walked out in the middle of the hour. LaVerne, at
last, burst into tears and, as if confessing something
she felt deeply ashamed of, admitted her intense loneliness and her equally intense fear of anyone's knowing of it.

Some people use feelings of shame as an excuse
not to confront their loneliness and share their
feelings with others.

THE EXPERT RELATER

A new breed of loneliness has arisen as a manifestation of the "age of psychology." Its victims make a fetish of their "psychological enlightenment" and act as if they were the in-group (one-upmanship) simply because they have undergone analysis or therapy. They claim to have learned to "let it all hang out" and in other ways play games of false openness, self-reliance, and even intimacy. Their "warmth" is readily demonstrated by their willingness to hug, kiss, and "relate" without fanfare or hesitancy. They may consider participation in a nude group as final evidence of their maturity.

Any endeavor, however great its nourishing potential, can be distorted into a toxic experience by those who are interested primarily in becoming more successful manipulators. In their hands, the potential for human growth through the psychotherapeutic arts becomes simply another tool of poisonous manipulation—of themselves or others. Growth and maturity are the legitimate goal of a genuine therapeutic experience. Instead, some people only learn more gimmicks which look like intimate relating but turn out to be games. As a result, the loneliness remains as intense as ever and is only briefly relieved by these experiences. Their daily lives remain empty, reflecting an absence of real integration and growth from their therapeutic experiences.

WHY NOT ASK?

Self-initiating behavior can create loneliness when carried to extremes so that it becomes a manifestation of greediness or a spoiled-child pattern. Some people insist that they are justified in asking others for anything they want. Often, people who have been in psychotherapy justify this attitude under the guise of "self-expression." This attitude reflects a lack of sensitivity about the poisonous effect it may have on others. An intimate relationship between two people begins to develop from their initial contact and is gradually shaped by their continuing pattern of relating. Regardless of how present-oriented a person may be, he is influenced by his past experiences in the relationship. The more an N person experiences the other as always asking for something, the more apt he is to withdraw or develop a "no" response as a prevailing counterattitude. The why-not-ask person is responsible for his greediness and its toxic effect on the relationship.

In an intimate relationship, aware people know each other's capabilities and limitations.

The caring person is aware of other people's limitations and avoids asking the impossible. Without such awareness, a partner in a meaningful relationship may bring about its destruction by greedily ignoring the limits of the other.

June and Jim met, fell in love, and decided to live together. June was more extraverted and full of energy. Jim was a graduate student who enjoyed solitude and preferred a few close friends. His parents were both dead and had left

him with sufficient income for both of them to
live on. He considered their living together a
"trial marriage" and hoped it was the beginning of
a lasting intimate relationship. June's attitude was
essentially "Why not?" They moved into an apartment building complete with swimming pool and
social-activities center.

Jim's studies were a full-time job, which he
took quite seriously. June enjoyed dabbling in all
kinds of activities and experiences. She was bright,
she had a college degree, and her interests
included pottery making, painting, and writing
poetry. She also enjoyed sports, all kinds of out-
door activities, and travel. She had no hesitation
in approaching strangers and quickly made
friends wherever she went. She seemed to enjoy
picking a person's brain for knowledge and information. Her barrage of questions was limited only
by the willingness of the other to answer. She
never seemed to have enough. For her, people
were like books: she would open them with curiosity, possibly find them of interest, finish with
them, and go on to the next one. At first, Jim
enjoyed the accounts of her daily experiences and
admired her ability to relate to people. She was
quite free in asking him for money, showing him
travel brochures, and talking about all the things
they could do together.

These activities were exciting to Jim also, but
June's continual requests began to burden him.
She would usually ask for something with the
phrase "Would it be possible for you to . . ."
Since almost anything June asked for was possible,
Jim would usually find himself nodding his head

in agreement, though often without any real enthusiasm.

About nine months after they had moved in together, a crisis developed. June, because of her frenzy of activities, was coming home later and later. Gradually, Jim began preparing more meals for himself. At times he would prepare something for the two of them and wait until she arrived. June seemed to appreciate this. One day June had another one of her "bright ideas." "Jim," she said, "since I'm so busy with all my activities that keep me away from the house and you're usually here studying, how would you feel about preparing all the meals?—so that you'll know just what you're going to have to eat, and it will be ready when you like it." Jim's outburst surprised both of them. "Goddammit, what are you contributing to this relationship? All I hear is 'Gimme, gimme, this is trippy and that's trippy.' I'm working for my degree and supporting you while you flit around doing what you damn please. And now you want me to cook for you."

June concluded that he was simply in a bad mood, shrugged her shoulders, and left for the evening. However, Jim had decided that henceforth when June approached him, he would deliberately focus on saying "no" even before he heard her request. At first she would walk away with an "Okay," as if he were in another grouchy mood and would soon get over it. When Jim, however, continued his stand against June's constant demands, she responded by going out with other men. She had told Jim of her intention, and he had no objection. For him, their relationship was already at an end. He had been drained by her "honest requests," and he asked her to move out. June was surprised and deeply hurt. Telling Jim that she was thinking of dating other men was simply one of her maneuvers which she thought would bring back his accepting, pliant attitude toward her. She still loved him deeply, but failed to understand that her asking had drained him and had become such a burden that it had suffocated his love.

After June moved out, she felt a deep longing and loneliness for Jim. Still perplexed about what had happened, she decided that she had been fooled and readily told everyone that Jim was really a bastard who "just got tired of me and kicked me out."

Greediness is greediness, no matter how justified or sophisticated. It wears out the "feeder."

While intimate human relationships are an essential source of nourishment, relating itself can be a way of generating loneliness when it has a poisonous effect on the self-nourishing capabilities within the person or on his partner.

CONCLUSION

The prime source of loneliness is within the person. He will be lonely to the degree to which he is fragmented and alienated from himself. He cannot substitute relations with other people for his own fragmented self, and this is exactly what the lonely person is most apt to spend his life trying to do. No matter how rich and gratifying a relationship may be, when a person seeks from others that which he needs to find within himself, he only creates a lonely, alienated existence. It is absurd to ask one person to take responsibility for another's loneliness, no matter how caring and loving that person might be. Further, this is the kind of manipulation that can ultimately destroy any relationship, however nourishing. When the responsibility for seeking one's own nourishment *and being* nourishing is neglected by one or both people, the deadly games of manipulation inevitably follow.

As long as a person insists on feeling victimized, he creates a stalemate for himself from which no change is possible. When he is willing to accept responsibility for what he does to himself, he opens himself to experimentation, risk-taking, and discovering more gratifying ways of being. Self-induced poisoning processes are based on fears and lack of confidence in one's own ability to do better. There is no guarantee of a painless antidote for loneliness. A person needs to discover how to activate his own capabilities. When a person's behavior becomes authentic and his actions are in good faith, he knows others are responding to him. His lifelong anxiety about being "found out" and his fears of rejection lessen as he gives up his false fronts. He becomes a more nourishing person.

We all respond to those who are nourishing, and genuinely nourishing people will not be lonely.

CHAPTER FIVE

Antidotes to Self-induced Toxic Behavior

Perhaps more than any other living organism, a human being is capable of doing something that he knows is not beneficial to his own well-being. He has enormous potential to poison himself intentionally. With full awareness of his needs, he often acts with deliberate force against himself. He is capable of literally choosing growth or death. The choice is his responsibility.

Self-induced patterns of poisoning include all attitudes or behavior initiated by the individual that disrupt his awareness and responsiveness to his needs. Other self-poisoning patterns disrupt the person's well-being when his most urgent needs are ignored or neglected while he devotes energy exclusively to his secondary needs—*i.e.*, those less vital to his over-all well-being.

If we are to stop poisoning ourselves, we must be aware of our experiencing self and in touch with what we are doing. When, for example, we discover that what we are doing is meaningless or irritating, we may attempt to terminate or minimize our toxic activities. Or, when we become aware that we are forcing ourselves to behave in a way that places excessive demands on our energy, we may check the purpose and necessity of putting ourselves through such ordeals.

Arthur was fanatical about not allowing anyone to take advantage of him. He would go to extreme lengths to rectify a situation in which he felt he had been mistreated. On one occasion, while traveling cross-country, he drove ten miles back to a market to return a container of cottage cheese when he discovered it was slightly sour. Typically he spent his money freely, even carelessly, but in such instances as this one, he insisted: "I won't be had even if I have to travel a hundred miles out of my way. I'm not going to let them get away with it!"

Many toxic patterns exist because we refuse to acknowledge the fact that we are the central initiator of our own behavior.

We would rather deny our toxic behavior than take responsibility for our own attitudes and actions. We would rather project the source of our discontentment onto others by placing the responsibility on the "its" and "theys" of the world, thereby perpetuating our self-poisoning process.

Allen enjoyed taking off in his camper for a weekend away from the city noise, smog, and congestion. Yet he became outraged at the Sun-

day-evening traffic jams as he returned home.
He fumed and fussed behind the steering wheel,
muttering curses and accusations at the other
drivers. At times he sounded as if the traffic jam
were a deliberate plot to irritate him. When his
wife attempted to calm him down, he turned his
rage on her. He refused to accept the responsibility for choosing to be in a traffic jam as an
inevitable part of his decision to go away for the
weekend.

Self-poisoning patterns persist when the person
ignores body expressions of toxic distress (discomfort,
tension, anxiety, etc.). He does not pay attention and
respond to them as indications of his needs. He is
not really interested in enhancing his self-awareness
and discovering how he may be causing his own discomfort. What he wants is to alleviate his distress any
way he can in the hope that somehow it will go away
and not recur. In essence, he is saying: "I am interested primarily in being comfortable. The pain of my
anxiety, fears, and apprehensions is some meaningless
torture that has no possible value and is at best a
nuisance and at worst a miserable curse."

Karen was a "good girl" who would do anything to avoid unpleasant scenes. She would insist
in all sincerity: "I can't stand to hurt anyone. It
makes me feel too guilty." For months she had
wanted to end the relationship with her boy
friend. Each time he called, she felt a pang of
annoyance in the pit of her stomach—an obvious
message that her body was spontaneously reacting to hearing from him—yet she refused to tell

him their relationship was over. When she could not think of an acceptable excuse, she would see him and even insist everything was fine between them. Her boy friend was unaware of her change of heart and attributed her moods to other problems. She persisted in her self-poisoning pattern not only by continuing a relationship she no longer wanted, but also by forcing herself to act as if she enjoyed it. Finally, her body could no longer tolerate her toxic game. One night in the middle of love-making she suddenly exploded—screaming that she couldn't stand to have him touch her and never wanted to see him again.

A person may be aware that his attitudes and behavior are unsatisfying, even painfully frustrating, yet fear to look too closely at his habitually ineffective ways of functioning. He may be aware of the impasse that has immobilized him, yet he will continue to avoid exploring possibilities of discovering a more nourishing existence. In spite of acknowledging that his fears are unreasonable, he may staunchly refuse to take any risks.

People frequently fantasize that giving up their poisonous but familiar patterns will leave them in an unknown vacuum that would be even more frightening. They choose to hang on to their ineffective behavior and resign themselves to despair and futility. Antidotes often involve letting go of attitudes and activities that have become obsolete (self-poisoning).

A person's ability to function effectively is disrupted when he ignores the processes of change within himself or his environment. Holding on to obsolete attitudes and behavior patterns means sacrificing one's flexibility and adaptability.

A person may delude himself into believing that he can avoid change and thereby maintain his inner security and stability. This delusion is particularly apt to occur when the major activities and circumstances of his life are relatively constant. When he feels secure in his job and has established a home, family, and routine of activities and living, he may indeed experience a sense of well-being and contentment. A nourishing attitude would include appreciation and joy about this stability. Yet life is never static, and there are always signs that change is occurring. A nourishing person fully appreciates the joys he experiences in the present.

Awareness of our continuing need to adapt to change need not detract from the gratifications and excitement of the present. Rather, they can be enhanced by the knowledge that we can continue to gratify our needs effectively by flowing with change.

Refusal to accept change is a commitment to fight an endless battle; it is a refusal to recognize the limitations of one's capabilities. The absurdity of refusing to recognize that life *is* change is carried even further by people who poison themselves in thinking that they can prevent change from occurring.

THE "DENIAL" OF THE SELF

A child is frequently taught that having "bad" thoughts, feelings, or impulses may cause him great harm. He learns to deny or block off these dangerous parts of himself. Human beings have a genius for denying the existence of major aspects of their identity. Some people haven't experienced for years what it feels like to be angry, to hate, or to cry. The psychic walls they have built and that may have existed for years continue to require a constant expenditure of energy to keep the suppressed needs from emerging. Occasionally, some kind of emotional explosion may occur. This cathartic effect is short-lived, and by the same process with which they built the walls initially they will again reconstruct them. For such T people, existence is an ongoing struggle against life forces within themselves which they see as evil. They insist that these parts of themselves are totally intolerable and would alienate them from others were they allowed expression. The person may live in a "volatile stalemate" in which he constantly struggles to maintain his equilibrium.

An effective antidote involves making contact with these alienated parts and allowing oneself to experience them. Only then can real change occur.

Denial of the self occurs whenever we refuse to recognize that our every thought, feeling, and action is a part of our selves. The poisoner wants to keep only the "good parts"—or at least, keep all others hidden. He has instigated an active process of fragmenting his self: *i.e.*, *dis*-integrating the unity and wholeness of his self. This fragmenting process is often apparent in the manner in which he expresses himself.

PATIENT: There is something down there that keeps wanting to come out. It scares the hell out of me.

THERAPIST: What do you mean by the "it" that's down there?

PATIENT: I think there's some anger down there.

THERAPIST: Would you be willing to "own" your anger by talking in the first person?

P: You mean, I have something down there—my anger is inside of me and I'm afraid to let my anger out.

T: Do you feel any different when you express yourself this way?

P: I feel more frightened—and I also feel a little excited.

T: Could you talk to your anger? What would you like to say if your anger could hear you?

P: Hello, anger. I know you're there. I've been afraid of you all my life. I'm afraid to let you come out. You scare the hell out of me.

T: Now could you give your anger a voice?

P: I'm your anger. I know you are scared of me. I'm really not so bad. I just need to come out now and then. If you weren't so afraid of me, you might even enjoy me sometimes.

T: Do you feel like responding to what your anger just said to you?

P: Okay, anger. I still don't trust you, but I'm willing to let you out a little and see what happens.

With this approach, the person begins again to make contact with this alienated part of himself. Now he can discover from his own experience (taking risks of his own choosing) whether the expression of his anger is as catastrophic as he has always imagined it would be.

RECLAIMING ONE'S PROJECTIONS

Frequently we may poison ourselves by projecting onto other people some quality in ourselves that we are unwilling to accept.

Phil imagined that people just didn't like him. For years he had convinced himself of this ("After all, people aren't exactly beating down my door to make friends with me"), and in this way he was able to avoid *his* fear of reaching out to people, and an even stronger fear that rejection would be overwhelmingly devastating to him. As he became aware of his own fearfulness, he began to cautiously consider taking some initiative. As frequently occurs, an antidote to a toxic pattern is often initiated when the frustration of an unfulfilled need becomes particularly strong. In this case, his best friend had given Phil his cousin's phone number. Phil had met her at a party a couple of months earlier and really wanted to know her better. He had been working up his

courage ever since: "Maybe I'll call her . . . on
the other hand, maybe she's going with somebody
by now. Maybe she's not even interested in me,"
etc. Phil's "great debate" with himself was simply
an expression of his inner fear. In one way or
another he continued to torture himself with inde-
cisiveness and conflict between his fearfulness
and what he wanted.

Antidote: "I am really interested in her, and I
feel anxious about taking the first step. I'm afraid
she will reject my overtures. If I stick my neck
out and call her and she rejects me, I'll feel even
worse—that would really hurt. I also feel that the
longer I wait, the more difficult I'm making it for
myself. I'll call her. I'm scared, *and* that's what I
honestly want to do."

Much self-poisoning is the result of refusal by the
person to accept those parts of himself which he feels
are undesirable, uncomplimentary, or disruptive to his
image of how he "should" be. A person always pays
the price when he rejects part of his self.

Phil's fear bothered him, so he tried to project it
onto the external world. As long as his fear remained
an alienated part of his self, he would continue to pay
the price by avoiding those people to whom he would
like to reach out.

Taking risks means reaching out in spite of
fears and anxieties. We cannot expect our anxieties to just disappear. Only *after* we experience
reaching out are anxieties and fears apt to
diminish.

THE TOXICITY OF THE PAST

Attitudes and behavior that may have been nourishing during earlier periods of one's life often become useless. Because they have become inappropriate or no longer effective in satisfying a person's needs, they must be discarded, or they become toxic and disruptive to present functioning. If a person allows this to happen, he perpetuates a poisonous process within himself.

To refuse to let go of the past is to deny the natural process of change that is a function of every living organism.

Holding on to obsolete experiences hinders new learning. The past is particularly toxic when it perpetuates fears and anxieties learned from earlier traumas that no longer fit present reality.

> Barry, as one of seven children, had to fight for attention from his parents, especially his father. Barry learned early how to move quickly into a dominant position and become the center of attention, for however brief a time. He used such precious moments to get in as much self-expression as possible. As a consequence, he learned to talk rapidly and without pause—lest he be interrupted by one of his rivals who also wanted their father's attention. He had discovered an effective behavior pattern—the best he could do to gratify his needs for a relationship with his father.

During his second year in college, Barry became aware that he had no close friends. He knew a great many people with whom he had superficial contact, but somehow his attempts at developing greater intimacy always seemed to fail. He discussed the matter with a school counselor, who suggested that he participate in an encounter group sponsored by the psychology department. In the encounter group he learned, for the first time in his life, how other people saw him.

"You come on too strong, man—I can't keep up with you."

"When you first came in, I thought to myself, 'Here's a guy I'd like to get to know,' but when you started rapping you sounded like a machine gun and you really turned me off."

"I resent your zapping into the center of attention every time there's a moment of silence."

"I like you, Barry, but I feel that if we were friends you wouldn't allow me enough space to express myself—you want to be the center of attention all the time."

Barry was startled by these comments. They were a revelation to him.

"I just didn't realize what I had been doing all these years. I remember Father would come home and sit down in his easy chair to relax and spend some time with us kids while we were waiting for dinner. I can see all seven of us clamoring around him, the little ones trying to get on his lap, the big ones trying to catch his eye. He tried to be fair about it and give us each a turn. I remember whenever my turn came I talked as fast as I could, trying to hold on to his attention by staring at him and making it as difficult as possible for him to tell me that my turn was up. It suddenly occurs to me that I'm still acting as if, every time I want to say something, six other kids are trying to shut me up so they can say what they want."

As an adult, Barry had continued to hold on to his fear that no one would allow him time for the self-expression he needed. He was holding on to an obsolete pattern, learned in the reality of his childhood, that was now becoming increasingly toxic. During his remaining time in the encounter group, Barry developed a sense of inner tranquillity. He actually found himself with very little to say, and for the first time in his life he began to enjoy listening to other people.

Human functioning that is dominated by past experience is almost invariably toxic.

The willingness to experiment with new behavior is a crucial aspect in discovering antidotes to obsolete toxic behavior patterns. In so doing, we are apt to find that long-standing fears and anxiety emerge in anticipation of some catastrophe. The antidote can be effective only when we discover for ourselves that the catastrophes we expect do not occur. It is in this experimental process that we may discover the falseness of our long-standing fears. The process of letting go has then begun. It may also happen in this experimental process that some ventures do not turn out to be gratifying and do indeed produce feelings of the kind that have frightened us in the past. Here too we may discover that the actual happening does not entail the expected disaster ("If I am rejected by someone I love I will be shattered forever").

Freedom from the past means letting go of what was *then*. The rejected lover may be initially discouraged when seeking new intimacy. He is disappointed that a new relationship is not immediately as fulfilling as what he felt with his lost lover. He is stuck in the past by the very act of comparing past and present relationships. Holding on to what is gone and no longer exists is always a self-poisoning process.

The grieving person needs to mourn when a love relationship ends in exactly the same sense in which one mourns the death of a loved one. Letting go of obsolete relationships (*e.g.*, death or rejection) begins with the person's willingness to recognize that he has lost someone important to him and to allow himself to mourn as deeply and as long as necessary. Interrupting one's mourning ("It's time to snap out of it") interrupts the "letting go" process so necessary to becoming emotionally available for new relationships.

Most funeral rituals have one purpose: confronting those who are left grieving with the fact of what *is*, so that they will be able to finish their letting go by mourning (accepting) their loss. The antidote to losing an intimate love relationship involves exactly the same process.

SPACE, PRIVACY, AND EXCLUSIVITY

Some needs exist that are characterized by a person's refusal to share with or in any way include others. Each of us has needs for space, ownership, and exclusive rights reflecting our nonsocial attitudes.

N people not only recognize the importance of these

needs for their over-all well-being: they appreciate this part of themselves as well. The cultural myths (how one should or should not be) often run contrary to these obviously self-centered aspects.

There are times and situations in which the mere presence of another human being can be a toxic intrusion. We may occasionally feel so "peopled-out" that the physical presence of anyone is experienced as toxic. In everyday living, the need for privacy is frequently something of which we deprive ourselves, through either lack of awareness or a self-poisoning attitude that it is "wrong" to want to be alone. Some people are embarrassed by their preference for living alone. Cultural mythology seems to have placed a taboo on a person's need for privacy and aloneness.

Each of us needs areas in our life sphere in which we feel we are entirely our own master, where we answer to no one but ourself. A person may experience this about a one-room apartment. Some feel this way toward their spouse and children. Even an inmate in a prison may choose a particular spot that he feels belongs exclusively to him.

Those who grew up in crowded quarters without a room of their own are often acutely aware of this need. They are resolute in their determination always to have some space of their own where no one else is allowed without their permission. A person's diary is a quite different example of the same basic need. Again, the same attitude is reflected in the rage a teen-age girl may experience when she discovers that Mother has cleaned her room *and* gone through her drawers. Her outrage is often an expression of deep emotional resentment that her private space has been ravaged. Parents who are unaware of similar needs in themselves often consider such outbursts as "silly" or "adolescent."

A lack of space poisons a person's sensitivity and responsiveness toward himself and other people; it is more difficult for him to appreciate his uniqueness. His creative potentials are stifled in a manner similar to what often happens to children raised in an institutional setting where they exist almost exclusively in groups and are treated like so many peas in a pod. When the vitality and excitement of experiencing one's uniqueness and exclusiveness is lacking, the person is most apt to become dull and empty. In extreme instances, the end product is a callused, insensitive human being who is also uncaring about and unresponsive to the needs of others.

Ronald's father was not only an Army colonel; he was a military officer in every aspect of his life style. His values centered on duty, responsibility, and "building strength and character." His wife served primarily as his orderly, and she feared him every bit as much as any private who served under him. He ran the house like a command post in the middle of a combat zone.

It was a foregone conclusion that Ronald would have a military career. At five, he was sent to one of the finest military schools in the country. He came home only for holiday vacations and part of each summer. At school he shared a room with three other cadets. All his possessions were periodically "open for inspection." He grew up not knowing what privacy meant. His "exclusive rights" were limited to a few personal possessions he kept hidden in his foot locker.

Ronald had been a "gentleman" as far back as he could remember. He not only lived by the book: he thought and felt by the book. By the time he entered high school (still in the military-school setting), even his voice was that of a soldier at attention talking to an officer. He had very little sense of identity or feeling of individuality. As a result of the atmosphere of the school, his attitude had always been one of self-protection and toughness, lest he be teased or ridiculed by his fellow cadets. He had observed this happening often enough: for example, when others were caught sobbing because they were homesick. He also witnessed teasing and ridicule when one of the more naïve cadets expressed anything that sounded warm, sensitive, or caring. The unfortunate cadet was subsequently referred to as "she."

Ronald even looked like his father. His proudest moment came when he was thirty and already a major, when his father looked at him one day and, in his typical officer's voice, said, "Son, you've turned out to be a chip off the old block; you're just like me. Congratulations!"

When a person feels poisoned by lack of sufficient space, he often spends his life trying to achieve it. People who grow up in the slums of a large city may struggle ceaselessly to get away from the spaceless environment of their childhood. Some leave for less populated communities. Others strive for economic success and the space this can purchase. In such instances, the need to establish a feeling of ownership of space and privacy may dominate their life style until they have reached their goal and satisfied their long-frustrated need.

DISCOVERING OUR FRUSTRATION INTOLERANCE

The chronic self-poisoner has little tolerance for pain—particularly the frustration endured when the gratification of a particular need must be delayed. Instead, he goes off half-cocked, solves the problem temporarily with a minimum of effort, but overlooks the real source of his tension. Over a period of time, the person's continual distress and frustration can become enormously draining. He won't mobilize himself sufficiently to put an end to the chronic problem that continues to sap his energy. T people who function this way typically have surges of enthusiasm in which they initiate activities and then lose interest before they have the satisfaction of seeing the task through to its conclusion.

Larry was earning a good salary. At twenty-five, thanks to credit buying, he had managed to accumulate a considerable number of material possessions, including an expensive sports car and a sailboat. While he enjoyed using his possessions, his enthusiasm was constantly dampened whenever he discovered a newer model he liked better. Consequently, he traded in his car and boat almost every year. The finance companies were delighted with him. "It's so neat, I've just got to have it!" he would exclaim.

One day his fiancée showed him by simple arithmetic that one fifth of his earnings went for interest on the things he was constantly buying. "You say we can't afford to get married on what you earn, yet you're working one day a week for the finance company." Larry was unable to avoid seeing his fiancée's logic, and agreed to stop buying things he didn't need and to pay off his accumulated debts.

His well-intended resolution was short-lived. He couldn't stand the gnawing temptation to buy what he wanted. He would not tolerate the frustration of depriving himself, even for another goal that he agreed was more important to him. Two years later he had extended his indebtedness to the brink of bankruptcy. His fiancée grew tired of his repeated broken promises and eventually broke off their engagement.

Feelings of tension or frustration are body messages of an existing need (Larry really wanted the things he bought). The self-poisoner has a choice: he can continue to expend his energies and resources, impulsively responding to every "itch," or he can learn to tolerate his frustration while directing his energies toward satisfaction of his more important needs, many of which may require a sustained effort before satisfaction is forthcoming.

Impulses are natural, healthy emotions which everyone experiences. For the nourishing person, the *expression* of various impulses is limited by reality and by other needs. The person who reacts impulsively and allows himself to be "carried away" usually lives a life style of chaos.

While the impulsive acting out of emotions may provide a great deal of momentary pleasure, it becomes toxic when the person allows his impulses to overwhelm him or ignores the consequences of his actions. Healthy expression is limited by the reality in which one is functioning at the moment. Impulsive behavior will inevitably violate reality as well as frustrate other needs within the person and the needs of others with whom the person is involved.

SPONTANEITY

Spontaneous behavior is not totally effortless. We often have to restrain conflicting needs so that our spontaneous expression can begin and we can avoid being interrupted. A writer, for example, frequently has to avoid distractions in order to set the stage for the spontaneous flow of his creative powers. He may have to remove himself from the usual distractions that would ordinarily compete with his need to write.

Spontaneity, then, is a matter of degree. Total spontaneity is an abstraction, except perhaps for relatively brief periods, since it implies a total absence of conflicting needs. Similarly, spontaneous action usually occurs within a context that presents external limitations on one's spontaneity. Spontaneous expression recognizes these limits, while impulsive expression recognizes no limits.

Inhibiting, even when reality demands it, has a toxic effect on the organism. Nourishing people seek to minimize their self-restraint and allow full self-expression.

Self-expression is limited only by their perception of the realistic consequences which require them to restrain their spontaneity.

NOURISHING AND TOXIC PAIN

Pain is a vital function necessary for survival. It is a feeling of distress which ranges from the discomfort of a pinprick to the chronic anxiety of a person who is phobic about life. While intense pain can constitute an unavoidable demand for urgent action, more subtle pains—especially those based on psychic needs—can be totally and permanently ignored.

The self-poisoner's attitude is that pain is "bad," unnecessary, and primarily something to get rid of as quickly as possible. Frequently he even refuses to accept the fact that he *is* in pain. Instead, he chooses to avoid his discomfort by distractions or by anesthetizing himself with drugs or alcohol. If he is willing to listen to his pain, he may discover what he needs to alleviate his discomfort. When he ignores this message, the frustrated need is apt to persist and intensify.

Anxiety, tension, apprehension, fearfulness, and other feelings are expressions of a person's state of emotional pain (and need). They always make a statement to the person if he is interested in listening.

In this sense, there is a potentially nourishing quality to pain which can direct us away from innumerable toxic experiences. It often tells us specifically what we need to avoid, eliminate, or otherwise respond to, either within ourselves or in our environment.

A dinner guest may have an intense dislike for the particular food his host is serving. He may feel nauseated as he attempts to eat it. If he chooses to ignore his pain (nausea), he induces further pain at the expense of his body. He has decided to ignore his pain and poison himself further out of his fear of others' reactions. For him a (painful) "good front" is more important than the comfort of his body. Such other-oriented attitudes are a hallmark of self-poisoners. They won't put themselves first even when doing so would not deprive anyone else of anything.

NOURISHING AND TOXIC PLANNING

Planning is apt to be more nourishing when we focus on the excitement of working toward our goal. Planning becomes more toxic when we concentrate on expectations for the future. Focusing on the future leaves us vulnerable to anxiety over the infinite possibilities of disappointment, failure, or catastrophe. Planning can range from a highly poisonous obsession with fears about the distant future to the realistic (nourishing) planning necessary to catching a plane on time. Part of our present existence may include an intense drive toward goals that cannot be achieved immediately and require long-range planning. This kind of planning can be frustrating, since it invariably requires postponement of other gratifications.

Each person *must* make commitments that are restricting to his present freedom. No one gets everything his way—nor does anyone ever *really* give up wanting it.

Planning is apt to become increasingly poisonous as it lessens a person's ability to experience his present life as meaningful and gratifying. Toxic planning is often an expression of fear of living. Anxiety about experiencing life may be so great that a person is constantly planning in order to avoid action or commitment to living in the present. If one so chooses, there are always excuses for postponing real gratification.

Earl's main game in life was making elaborate plans for the future at the expense of the present. He had a good job, and his income easily equaled that of his friends. Yet he kept complaining that he could not afford to buy a home and raise a family while his friends were able to do this. He was jokingly referred to as the "community miser" and was frequently ridiculed for his stinginess.

For years Earl had been investing his money in stocks and would explain to his wife that his investment program would assure their future and that of their children. He was very secretive about this and would dream of the day he would reveal his wealth to his friends. Often frustrated, particularly about not having children, his wife would persistently challenge him, and a violent argument would ensue. Earl continued to have his way.

When Jean was thirty-five, her physician advised her that if she wanted a family (particularly since they both planned on three children), they had best get on with it. Under this pressure, Earl agreed that it was time for Jean to become pregnant. Then the unexpected occurred (one of the toxic aspects of living excessively in the future): Jean was unable to conceive. She went the usual route of fertility specialists for two years, yet was unable to become pregnant. She began to approach Earl with the possibility of adopting children, but he adamantly refused. He was determined to have a family of his own.

When Jean reached forty, she told Earl that either they would adopt a child, since she had given up hope of having her own, or she would leave him. Earl was now forty-five and over the past five years had become angry and bitter at Jean's failure to meet his expectations. He refused to take any responsibility for the current situation. He was willing to concede that he had erred in waiting too long, but he refused to compromise on the adoption issue, and they were subsequently divorced.

Earl represents the attitude T people take toward the goals they seek. Their overwhelming motivation is to achieve the goal, regardless of the destructive effects of the process on their well-being. They may compulsively drive themselves while ignoring the effects of their compulsion. T people often fear that if they let up in their frenzied pursuit of future goals, their lives will be chaotic or empty.

Toxic planning is exemplified also by those who overemphasize success. This attitude contaminates their ability to experience the process of living their lives. Some would gladly take a pill that would render them unconscious until they reached a certain goal. While this may be sensible for a person undergoing surgery, it is something else when a student exclaims, "I wish I could go to sleep and wake up four years from now with my degree." A vacationer speeds along the highway in order to arrive at his destination as quickly as possible. A child gulps down his food so that he can get back to the television set.

In such cases, the process of being alive is not only unappreciated and unenjoyed, but even perceived as a tedious, painful part of living which must be tolerated. The most obvious poisonous effect of excessively goal-oriented planning is that it may render most experience meaningless. The student is not interested in the *process* of his learning or his experience as a student. The child is not interested in *tasting* his food. The traveler is not interested in the beauty of the area *on his way* to his destination. The experiences that occur while we work toward goals *are* frequently a major part of our lives.

Achievements tend to be short-lived in the emotional nourishment they provide when they are accomplished. End-oriented people poison themselves by compulsively focusing on a new goal as soon as the previous one is reached. For them, life without future goals is a sterile, empty existence. If a person is unwilling to see the nourishment in the *process* of living and working, it is even less likely that he can allow himself to experience the nourishment of "doing nothing" and simply enjoying himself without pushing on again toward a new goal.

Toxic planning is commonly found in people who tenaciously cling to a job that is meaningless and boring for the security it will provide in old age. Satisfaction in the long-cherished goal of not being forced to work for a living is apt to be short-lived. At retirement, the individual finds himself confronted with the absence of a day-to-day meaning. He never took the time to learn how to live. His "achievement" has led him down a blind alley.

N people, even in their long-range planning, continue to focus *primarily* on being in touch with their ongoing experiences.

N people continue to find excitement and interest in the present regardless of their age and regardless of the unavoidable restrictions placed on their activities by physical limitations, cultural attitudes, or other circumstances. They have discovered the simple process of self-generated interest. They *allow* their attention to focus on the unfolding now.

The desire to realize one's potentials can be extremely gratifying. A nourishing attitude toward these needs focuses on the process of growth rather than the accomplishment of reaching some end point of achievement. An artist may experience gratification and nourishment with each creative work he produces. He may be well aware of his dissatisfactions as well as his gratifications and may strive to improve. While he wants to be more effective in expressing himself, he also appreciates his creativity in his present efforts. With a nourishing attitude, the quest for excellence is a self-validating experience. The person enjoys his efforts in the process of working toward his goal. The athlete feels satisfaction about his day's workout. He feels good about his performance regardless of where he happens to be in terms of reaching his athletic ambitions. He nourishes himself in the process rather than becoming obsessed with his ultimate goal.

ORGANISMIC DISCHARGE

The term "organismic discharge" expresses a dramatic release of accumulated tensions. As such, it can have enormous value in subsequently re-establishing a more natural balance between the person's needs for spontaneity and for control. The possible kinds of organismic discharge are usually limited to *some* experiences of joy, grief, rage, sexual orgasm, and vomiting. Usually the emotional aspects of these five kinds of experiences are responsive to a specific, more immediate situation. While they may make one feel better temporarily, they do not have the intensity and pervasiveness necessary to relieve long-standing chronic tension.

Self-poisonous patterns, particularly those which have continued for a considerable length of time, gradually create an accumulated tension in various areas of the body. These are the "squeezes" that literally make the body tight and rigid—impair its natural, relaxed functioning.

Psychic self-poisoning gradually erodes physical health and eventually contributes to physical illness or impairment.

When a person inhibits himself from allowing the full expression of his emotions (when there is no realistic reason in the *present* situation to do so), he poisons himself to that extent. Most T people, when they laugh, cry, or get angry, can be observed squeezing themselves at the same time. Their laughter frequently sounds squeezed; they put their hands over their mouth or hide their face; they even cut off their laughter as quickly as possible. Others sound more as if they are choking when they cry. Similarly, T people —with or without awareness—squeeze down their full body expression during sexual orgasm, particularly their vocal utterances and noises.

An organismic discharge is an emotional expression that erupts spontaneously and completely dominates the person. It literally overwhelms him with its power as it mobilizes the entire body into involuntary action. Such intense emotional reactions cannot be willed or deliberately instigated. They either occur spontaneously or do not occur at all. Like a seizure, they run their course until the discharge of energy is completed. They are singularly valuable in eliminating the toxic effects of accumulated tensions and elicit a subsequent expansion of awareness and contact with the environment. The discharge of energy that occurs with these experiences may melt psychic walls that have blocked healthy functioning for years. Afterward, the person immediately feels more alive, more in touch with his senses, and unusually aware of himself and his environment.

A well-integrated person, one who is fully accepting of all his human qualities, is capable of experiencing all five modes of organismic discharge. He lets the experience happen and, rather than attempt to resist or dampen his reaction, gives in to it fully and *allows* it to take over his whole being.

T people experience fright, even panic, when they become aware of feeling emotion that threatens to burst into expression so intensely. Frequently they equate such an experience with "going crazy."

Joy has the quality of an organismic discharge when the person's feelings of excitement and exhilaration consume his entire attention. He loses all self-consciousness and fear of embarrassment. This is most readily apparent in children who literally jump with joy and scream with delight. No words are adequate or spontaneous enough to fully express the intensity of their feelings. Adults who allow themselves to be carried away with laughter are usually aware that this kind of joy has taken over. They literally "can't stop laughing" as their whole body shakes involuntarily. Again, such experiences of joy are followed by a relaxed, open, tension-free feeling.

Sometimes a person laughs with an overwhelming joy of relief when he discovers how he has been poisoning himself. A sudden insight of awareness of how he may have been oppressing himself for years may elicit a discharge of laughter that melts the grimness of his attitude toward himself and living.

Perhaps the most obvious organismic discharge is sexual orgasm, which is also an involuntary bodily reaction that, once it starts, takes over the entire body until the orgasm is completed. What is less obvious is that the intensity and pleasure of an orgasm varies greatly in the feeling of completeness and satisfaction a person experiences. Full sexual discharge often occurs in a person after years of limited orgasms. For various reasons—gradual loss of inhibition, a more intense love relationship, etc.—the person may be astonished at his own ability to respond so totally ("I never knew sex could be like that!"). Full sexual discharge also brings with it a melting of general tensions and a subsequent state of relaxation and openness. In nourishing love relationships, this is also reflected in a growing mutual trust and intimate sharing. While lovers may enjoy talking with each other for hours, in a nourishing relationship they also can enjoy sharing periods of silence and nonverbal relating. They don't feel they need to do something. They can enjoy the temporary state of relatively full satisfaction and completeness that frequently follows an intense sexual experience.

PSYCHOLOGICAL VOMITING

Priscilla was a virgin when she married Luther. Her sex education had been limited to understanding the menstrual process and the physiology of conception, pregnancy, and childbirth. She trusted Luther implicitly, and he was able to alleviate her sexual anxieties by his reassurances that he had "been around."

During their honeymoon, Luther was totally impotent. His inability to attain an erection completely mystified Priscilla. Luther assured her that it had never happened before and that the "problem" would work itself out. As the months went by, they gradually evolved a satisfactory sex relationship through mutual masturbation. Still, whenever they attempted intercourse, Luther would lose his erection.

Somewhat ingeniously, he managed to impregnate Priscilla by entering her at the instant he began to have an orgasm through masturbation. In this way, they conceived two children.

As Priscilla's sexual anxiety lessened, she became increasingly dissatisfied with her sex life. She suggested they seek professional help—but Luther angrily refused. As she became more persistent, he became increasingly angry and, in an explosive argument one day, told Priscilla that it was her fault; that he had been to bed with lots of girls and this had never happened; that there was something lacking in *her*.

This absolutely devastated Priscilla, and she never brought up the subject again. She continued to live feeling herself to be only half a woman, convinced that she lacked some mysterious quality to arouse men sexually.

Priscilla became confused when Ralph, a close friend of Luther's, began to flirt with her at social gatherings. It took several months for Ralph to persuade Priscilla to secretly meet him for lunch. Afterward she was astonished at her own sexual excitement when they indulged in mild petting in his car. Despite her fears that Ralph too would be impotent with her, Priscilla agreed to go to bed with him. A whole new world opened up! Ralph had no difficulty having intercourse with her.

Priscilla's ecstasy shortly changed into rage against Luther. She confronted him with the fact that she had had an affair and the man had found her wholly desirable. Priscilla's fury was so intense that she simply overwhelmed his anger about what she had done. "I don't give a damn how angry you are. You've been lying to me all these years.

You convinced me that I was lacking as a woman!
You weren't man enough to face your own problem. You disgust me so I could vomit."

Priscilla's repulsion toward Luther became
increasingly intense. For weeks she refused even
to sleep in the same room with him. She was
absolutely repelled by any gesture of physical contact from him. The situation was, of course,
intolerable. Finally Luther agreed they needed
professional help, and both went into therapy
separately. Priscilla's rage at Luther, she found,
and her disgust at what he had perpetrated
against her, was something to which she could
not reconcile herself. Six months later, she asked
him for a divorce.

**Psychological vomiting is a sudden release of a
toxic attitude or behavior pattern that the person
has swallowed and that remains, like a foreign
object, unassimilated within him.**

This often occurs when a person suddenly becomes
aware of the immensity of a particular toxic pattern or
relationship. His new awareness may be so intense
that his body is repulsed by the thought of continuing
this process one moment longer. It is a dramatic way
of finishing an unfinished situation. In psychotherapy,
this is frequently described as a sudden "break-
through," which is followed by an abrupt and lasting
change in the person's behavior or functioning.

An infant readily regurgitates whatever he is unable to digest. This is a natural process of eliminating

something toxic, and he feels better afterward. As he grows older, he usually becomes increasingly reluctant to vomit, even when his body sends a clear message that this is what he needs. He has been taught to force the poison to remain in his system. He has also learned to do the same thing on the psychic level. Most adults, rather than appreciate the value of psychological vomiting, ignore their need to "throw up" toxic experiences. What cannot be assimilated must be eliminated or the person poisons himself.

A willingness, even eagerness, to vomit up unacceptable, poisonous experiences is a valuable antidote process.

The adult world usually breaks down the natural antidote of the disgust-expulsory process against psychological toxicities. Very young children will "swallow" anything rather than risk the loss of parental love. They learn to repress their spontaneity and retain the poison. The adult is not in this vulnerable position. He is free to rediscover his "disgust signal system," appreciate it, and listen to it. His disgust can again resume its natural function of avoiding new poison and telling him what (or whom) he needs to regurgitate.

When a person becomes aware that he is holding on to an attitude or pattern which he now experiences as disgusting, he can begin to let go of it. He may experience his feeling of disgust so intensely that he literally needs to vomit. Long-standing poisonous patterns can be melted by a giving-in to one's need to vomit with an awareness of what is being expelled with the vomiting.

THE NOURISHMENT OF WITHDRAWAL

Withdrawal can rejuvenate "psychic" energy in the same way in which sleep alleviates physical fatigue. Unwillingness to withdraw is usually a manifestation of anxiety about being alone and isolated from others. Contacting one's "inner fortress" is of paramount importance in discovering one's potentials for greater self-reliance. The nourishment of withdrawal is part of each person's self-regulating capacity for coping with the stresses of living. Phobic attitudes against accepting aloneness prevent the person from discovering and appreciating the many psychological processes that rely totally and solely on his inner potentials. When he is alone or isolated from others who are unavailable or cannot give him what he needs, his only real contact is with himself and the natural world in which he lives. The ability to withdraw from others and experience this feeling of contact offers enormous potentials for self-nourishment, even where one's very survival is at stake.

CENTERING

A person may lose touch with his basic needs as well as the way in which they relate to what he actually does in his ongoing existence. The more fragmented he becomes, the more apt he is to experience confusion, bewilderment, or feelings of not knowing who he is. While his existence is not necessarily meaningless, his behavior lacks integration.

"Centering" constitutes a balance between opposing behavior patterns. When we center our lives, we integrate these opposites into a harmonious flow, providing the contrast that makes our lives exciting and meaningful.

A person who is centered is more aware and more accepting of the range of potential behavior or feeling of which he is capable. For example, he may be in touch with his aggression-passivity dimension (a purely arbitrary descriptive term) and be aware of and comfortable with his experiencing of intense rage and more moderate anger and resentment, as well as feelings of complete passivity. Further, he is able to experience all of these emotions and accepts all of them as part of himself.

T people do not necessarily live their lives in agony or torture. Often their toxic patterns have the effect of making their lives uninteresting. While they may rarely feel despair, they also rarely feel enthusiastic or excited. The chronic self-poisoner simply has so much energy locked into obsolete attitudes and behavior that he lacks the vitality necessary to experience contrast and variation in his living.

One of the most significant characteristics of N people is awareness of their "center" and their ability to maintain contact with it.

N people are more quickly and intensely aware of when their life style is deviating from their "center." T people, in contrast, lack a center, remain dis-integrated, and may never be truly in touch with who they really are. Their lives consist of a conglomerate of styles. They latch on to chunks of other people's attitudes and behavior patterns that seem to provide them with some meaning.

The "conglomerate life style" of T people creates an atmosphere of semi-chaos. They themselves rarely know what they will be "into" next. Since they lack a center of their own, they have to copy from others, but what they take from another person is never really assimilated, and it fails to provide them with a feeling of real meaning and purpose.

The emptying process can be a powerful antidote when a person is willing to take a good look at his life style.

Emptying provides him with the opportunity to check out which attitudes and behavior patterns reflect his own center and which represent "other-oriented qualities." Even T people are reluctant to confront themselves with the possibility that they are not their own person.

Dan was forty-six when he broke his back in an auto accident and was immobilized for months. After several weeks, his resentment and agitation over his forced confinement became so intense that his physician warned him that he was jeopardizing his recovery. He gradually lapsed into a mild depression. He felt abandoned, despite the interest and concern of his family and friends. He became more introspective and began to take stock of himself and his life. Much of what he had been intensely involved in seemed unappetizing, boring, and even irrelevant to what he now felt he wanted. Looking back, he saw how his life style had shifted according to changing outside forces.

During Dan's college days, his best friend was a political radical who attacked "big business" incessantly. Dan found himself joining his friend's political activities on campus while at the same time majoring in business administration and hoping for a career with a large corporation.

After graduating, and through the considerable influence of his family, Dan obtained a job as a junior executive in a large manufacturing company. His colleagues would suggest to Dan in a friendly manner that he find a suitable girl and settle down. He consequently found himself evaluating his girl friends as potential wives instead of allowing relationships to develop naturally. He recalled feeling as if he had just been accepted into a fraternity when Sue, the daughter of a vice-president of a large corporation, agreed to marry him.

When Dan and Sue were married, they had intended to rent a small house at the beach, away from most of their social and business friends, but Dan's new father-in-law, a warm, persuasive man, convinced Dan that "the right neighborhood" was important for his future. Furthermore, he happened to know of a perfect house. They moved into the house three months later. Dan enjoyed the business world, cared a great deal for Sue, and soon felt comfortable in their new home. He appreciated the advice and suggestions offered by more experienced people which at the time he felt really furthered his own interest.

"Come on, Dan, you can at least *try* golf—lots

of people enjoy it, you know." This was his
brother-in-law's way of persuading him that golf
provided many more opportunities for business
contacts and had a lot more going for it than
Dan's preferred camping trips. Dan tried golf,
liked it, and soon developed some skill. Again,
there was nothing crucial about changed preference in recreation. A few years later, he bought
a boat on the same basis. He had wanted a sailboat, but again found himself persuaded to buy a
more luxurious, far more expensive cabin cruiser.
"I have to admit I like the cabin cruiser," Dan
jovially confessed a few months later. His well-
meaning friends congratulated him on his intelli-
gent decision (meaning he liked what they
liked).

These and countless other similar experiences
went through Dan's mind repeatedly as he lay
confined during his convalescence. He wondered
if he and Sue might not have developed a more
intimate marriage had they spent a year or two
alone at the beach. He wondered how he would
feel pitting his navigating skills with a sailboat
against the wind and the sea. He knew he preferred his camping trips to golf. He felt a growing
irritation with his willingness to follow the advice
of others and his own failure to take the time to
see for himself what he really wanted.

Dan's accident had forced him into a situation
in which he was away from his usual rush of activities and interests. Now he felt a painful void,
knowing that he could not, nor would he be willing to, simply pick up the same routine after his
recovery. He was both depressed and outraged

to discover that "At age forty-six, I don't know who the hell I am."

Dan is an example of a conglomeration of other people's interests and values. In order to discover his own center, he first had to become aware that his life style was not his own creation. Sometimes, as in Dan's case, a situation forces a person into a void. When this occurs, one can simply agonize about his plight, or something of real value may emerge.

N people allow themselves time to evaluate their lives and make sure their decisions have been made to please themselves.

Finding one's center is an evolving process rather than something one suddenly discovers. The willingness to do nothing and cut off external stimuli sets the stage for greater contact with one's self. When a person is intensely in touch with himself, he automatically cuts off the processes that would normally distract him from his state of being at the moment. When he is intensely involved with his experiencing self, other activities may cease or even be impossible. When, for example, a person is talking, he may be so overwhelmed by the welling up of his emotions that he is unable to continue and must stop trying to talk until the intensity of his feelings diminishes.

Sometimes even a few hours of emptiness can enable us to get more in touch with our center. It is a kind of psychic sleep in which a maximum amount of our energy is at rest and available, *and* we are aware

of this. We may see the absurdity or futility of much
of what we do and actually laugh at our self's breaking
through our unawareness.

SIMPLIFYING

Living one's life in the now is simple—it is not easy.
A person usually lives inundated in the debris of past
experiences. His activities may largely reflect his need
to compensate for past failures. Or, he complicates his
life by attaching value judgments to everything he
does. Each activity is essentially a reaction to his past
in one way or another. Ironically, in his doing so, the
clutter and complexity of his life increases rather than
diminishes. He continues to contaminate what he does
in the unfolding now. Today becomes the past of
tomorrow with still more new, unfinished business.

**N people are able to enjoy the richness of experi-
ence that full awareness of relatively simple life
styles can provide.**

Simplifying means being more discriminating and
selective about activities and relationships. It also
means becoming more discriminating in our responsiveness to our environment. It is obviously toxic to
flood ourselves with more stimulation than can be
assimilated. Any gratifying experience becomes toxic
when it is excessive. Awareness itself can be excessive
when it introduces more stimulation and excitement
than the organism is capable of absorbing. "Psychic
earplugs," "psychic blindfolds," and other ways of

limiting input are an essential part of the antidote to an overcomplicated (toxic) way of living. Greedy people are often so intent on taking in as much as they can—food, experience, relationships—that they miss the richness that one can fully experience only by focusing on one thing at a time and staying with that experience until it is finished.

Simplifying means taking greater responsibility for how one responds to experiences. When a person is irritated by a rude salesman, he may decide to use up a half hour of his life "ventilating" his feelings. It is his responsibility if he chooses to expend his time and energy in this manner.

A person attempting to maintain several intimate relationships may discover that he is exhausting himself in the process. While each relationship may be meaningful, all of them together may demand more time and energy than he has available. Some people don't know when to stop. They allow their greediness to drive them into an increasingly complex existence, much as a young child turned loose in a candy store indulges until he makes himself sick. Quantity rarely equals the richness of a single but deeply felt experience.

PLAY

One of the most delightful aspects of being alive is play. Its central role in the living of a vital life is often underestimated. Without exception, people need play. A lack of appreciation of the need and joy of play is a dominant attitude of those whose lives are lopsided with work, the "burden" of responsibility, and the deadly toxic attitude that life is "serious business."

Play is a release of tension and a source of unlimited creativeness. It energizes the person and
enables him to function more effectively and
joyfully in other activities.

Under conditions of stress, play is the first thing that
T people give up. The anxious person usually lives in
a continuous state of fantasized crisis in which he
decides that his well-being is too tenuous for him to
allow himself the "luxury" of play.

T people suffocate their spontaneity with the fantasy that they cannot afford time away from work and
chores. Instead, they grind away, insisting that staying
alive means work and rest in an unending cycle.

The more mature the self-poisoning adult feels he
must appear, the less he is apt to allow himself any
playfulness. This is exemplified in the compulsive businessman whose anxious wife waits and hopes that her
husband will come to his senses before it's too late.
When her husband does take a vacation, it is frequently more of a rest cure to recover from a state of
exhaustion. Rarely is adult play viewed as a primary
need in life.

Perhaps the most powerful antidote for avoiding
and minimizing toxic experiences is an appreciation of our aliveness.

CONCLUSION

The nourishing person centers his awareness on his
joy, excitement, and satisfactions. His attitude toward

life emphasizes his determination to savor and relish to the fullest what he finds satisfying about himself and others.

The N person selects what dissatisfactions with himself and his world he wishes to modify. Only when toxic patterns are sufficiently disruptive to his growth and well-being does he become interested in initiating change. He simply tolerates many of the inevitable poisonous aspects of living. He responds to disturbing experiences and feelings by "listening" and deciding how urgent or realistic it is for him to attempt to alleviate his discomfort. He is aware that pain and distress are inevitable, and he has no intention of trying to eliminate them. He seeks the simplest antidotes that are appropriate.

While there is no growth without pain (*e.g.*, the anxiety of taking risks), the presence of pain is no assurance that one is growing. Frustrating relationships or a frustrating way of using up one's life often result in futile pain from which a person may continue to suffer indefinitely.

Antidotes require awareness of when suffering is unnecessary.

When a person becomes sufficiently fed up with chronic suffering, his pain may then begin to take on a nourishing quality. Only when he is sufficiently aware of his suffering will a person motivate himself to experiment with new behavior patterns. Pain is nourishing when it encourages the person to take risks to expand the dimensions and potentials of his existing self. This is how he learns to become more nourishing and to minimize his toxic experiences.

It is each person's choice and responsibility whether he is interested in giving up or modifying his toxic patterns. A person may have strong objections to letting go of his self-poisoning. He may be convinced that it is necessary. The discovery that most squeezing in of one's self is unnecessary may not come easily; it may not come at all. Any attempt to alleviate self-poisoning remains ineffective as long as the antidote makes no real sense or is too frightening. A person may at times be coerced into letting loose. Sufficient encouragement from others may seem to be of help. Alcohol or drugs may short-circuit his toxic attitude. None of these experiences is effective as a real antidote to the self-poisoning process. None frees his energies for growth and integration. Only when the person genuinely feels that a toxic attitude or behavior pattern no longer makes sense, and he is willing to experiment with giving it up, can an antidote be effective.

CHAPTER SIX

Nourishing and Toxic Relating

Cues indicating when relating is nourishing and when it is toxic appear constantly. When a person is aware, he can feel the N and T qualities in his relating to the other. Although a person's behavior is always a mixture of nourishing and toxic qualities, each of the statements in the following dialogues is predominantly N or T.

1. HE: Hi, my name's George. I saw you in class yesterday and I knew I wanted to meet you.
   SHE: Thank you, but I'm really not interested.

N & T Evaluation:

HE: N

George is making a straight statement, clearly asking for what he wants and sharing part of himself at the same time ("I admired you yesterday").

SHE: N

She gives an honest answer without defending, explaining, or justifying her lack of interest in knowing George. She presumably is honestly not interested in George, for whatever her reasons may be. She chooses to be direct and to the point and leaves George to handle his own hurt feelings. Explanations or excuses that might leave George feeling a little better about being rejected are likely to lead to further persistence on his part and a subsequent toxic dialogue.

2. Boss (*over the intercom to his secretary*): Nancy, will you please come in? I have a few letters to dictate.

   SECRETARY: You asked me to go to the bank and the post office as soon as possible, and I was just on my way out.

   Boss: I know, but I want to get these letters off my mind. You can go to the bank after I finish dictating.

   SECRETARY: I feel annoyed at your lack of consideration for me. I'm doing what I thought you wanted and was all set to finish one thing before I start another. Now you want me to do something else instead. That's what makes me all up-tight about working for you.

   B: I don't intend to hassle you. I just opened my mail and need to respond to some important letters.

   S: I would appreciate your being willing to wait until I get back from the bank and the post office.

   B: I'll run my office my way, not yours. Now come in here right away.

   S: Okay. But I resent your authoritarian attitude.

N & T Evaluation:

Nancy's attitude is essentially toxic. She wants to do "her own thing" in a context in which her freedom is realistically restricted. While it is reasonable to ask for what she wants, her insistence is inappropriate to the reality of the situation.

The boss's attitude is nourishing. He is honestly putting himself first in doing what he needs rather than playing "nice guy" and creating more tension for himself. In this situation he is an authoritarian figure who has real power over her and, unless he chooses to poison himself, is willing to assert that power when he feels he is being unreasonably opposed.

Another essential point of this dialogue is that the context is one which is not primarily a personal, intimate relating. Rather, the boss and the secretary are working for economic reasons. How well they actually relate as two individuals is of secondary importance in this setting.

3. MOTHER *(to her twenty-year-old son)*: Did you enroll in school yet, like you said you would?

SON: Not yet. I haven't decided whether I'm ready to go back.

MOTHER: You've been out for a year. I should think that would be time enough for you to know what you want.

SON: Don't hassle me. I'll go back when *I'm* ready and not until.

M: I don't want to nag you about it. You already know how much your father and I would like to see you return to school and continue your studies. I'm sorry if I don't sound pleasant and casual about it, but I don't feel that way.

S: Okay, okay. I get the point. Now get off my back.

M: All right, I'll drop it. However, your father and I have decided that if you're not going back to school, we feel you should get a job and support yourself. After all, you're a twenty-year-old adult.

S: What is this—some kind of blackmail game: either I go back to school or I get kicked out?

M: No, it's not a blackmail game. We both love you very much and want to do whatever we can for you. However, now that your brother has graduated from college and is working, and your sister is married, your father and I feel that when you have finished your education we would like to sell the house. We have some plans of our own to travel, and I would like a smaller place that's not so hard to keep up.

S: That sounds very cozy. What are you trying to do—make me feel guilty? That you're depriving yourselves for my sake? You'll do anything to get me to go back to school. Well, I'm not going till I get ready. I may *never* go back. I'm going to show you *and* Dad that nobody can push me around.

N & T Evaluation:

The mother's attitude is essentially nourishing. She and her husband have plans, but at the same time she states that they are willing to cooperate if he decides to go back to school. She is also expressing her own (selfish) needs and plans. Further, the mother is frank in admitting that she would like to see her son continue his education.

The son's attitude is essentially toxic. His comments suggest inner conflicts and anxieties which he has not resolved and which he readily dumps on his mother. He is not interested in her point of view. The most toxic attitude of the son is his defiant, rebellious attitude against his parents. He seems ready to poison himself by proving a point that they can't make him do anything, and he places this ego trip ahead of confronting himself with deciding what is best for him.

In one's personal existence, rebellion against another is usually a toxic attitude. The rebel has given over his power to someone else (another self-poisoning process) and then decides that this superior enemy which he himself has created is his main obstacle.

---

4. WIFE: I don't know how to tell you this except to come right out with it. I'm leaving you. I want a divorce.

HUSBAND: Wow—you could have hit me with a baseball bat and it wouldn't have hurt as much. I don't know what to say—I can't believe it.

WIFE: This is not some sudden decision of mine. I've been thinking about it for months. For a long time I haven't felt that we really shared much. You're so busy, you work such long hours, and when you come home you're exhausted. I feel like anything I need from you is just an added burden. Usually when I ask you for something you tell me you're too tired and you go to bed. I just feel empty, unloved, uncared for, and I want more for myself.

HUSBAND: I've been working hard so that we can really do what we want. I thought you knew I was working hard so that I could give you everything you needed.

W: I don't need all those material things. They're nice, I enjoy them, but I'm lonely. I need a relationship; I need to be able to share myself with someone, and you're not available.

H: We've got eight years invested in this marriage. We have been building something—surely you'll agree on that. I know I've been neglecting you, and I know I've been putting in too much time for my business. But I'll be different. I don't want to lose you.

W: That's what your usual answer has been when I've told you how I feel. And that's been going on for years. It's very important for *you* to be a success and make a lot of money. I feel you would resent me if you gave up working the way you want to work because I'm dissatisfied.

H: You're much more important to me. I promise you things will be different. I promise you I will not work after six o'clock any night. I also promise you that I won't take on any weekend meetings or invite business associates for a social occasion and then talk business. I'll stop all that. Just give me another chance.

N & T Evaluation:

The wife's attitude is essentially a nourishing one. She has been sending clear signals to her husband about her frustrations and discontentments without giving him an ultimatum. Her attitude is also nourishing in the sense that her conversation reveals an awareness of her need to make a painful decision about which she has considerable conflict. She cares for her husband and is aware that simply caring for him is not sufficient to provide her with the nourishment she needs. In her dialogue, she avoids blaming or making demands and instead comes to him with her decision. She is also responsive to his reaction, although skeptical, and maintains a flexible attitude, being aware that, in the past, possibly he really hasn't heard how strongly she feels about their lack of relationship.

The husband's attitude is essentially toxic. He seems to have lost his perspective in not providing himself and his wife with a nourishing life style that is responsive to a broader range of emotional needs.

The most toxic aspect of the husband's conversation is his well-meant promise to "be different." (The road to hell is paved with good intentions.) Despite his caring and sincerity, if he gives up his obsessive approach to his business on the basis of fear that his wife will leave him, he will generate an underlying resentment that he must "pay her

*off" in this way to maintain the relationship. One
way or another, he will express this resentment.
His other self-poisoning pattern is predicting the
future in terms of promises that he cannot possibly know he will be able to sustain on an ongoing
basis.*

Whenever a person programs himself to behave
a certain way in the future, he begins a self-
poisoning process.

A more nourishing (and realistic) attitude would
be a statement of intent that he will work toward
becoming more aware of his wife's needs and his own
needs other than his business and strive to lessen his
obsession with financial success. This is a more realistic antidote in that it recognizes the power and emotional investment he has in his work.

The resolution of such conflicts is a process.
Promises are poison, despite a person's sincerity
and best intentions at the time he makes them.
Like New Year's resolutions, it is only a question
of how long a person can manipulate himself
before his real needs again emerge.

---

5. KATHY: I'm angry at you for leaving me alone at
the party last night. You know I don't know
many people, and . . .

TIM: I was just saying hello to some of my friends. I saw you talking to some people, and I didn't know you were alone.

KATHY: I was talking to someone for a while. But he left, and . . .

TIM: I'm sorry that I didn't keep an eye on you every moment. I really didn't know you were alone.

K: I told you before that I don't feel you see me as an individual person, that you . . .

T: Now, that's unfair to make that generalization. I know I was wrong last night, and I apologize. I will try to be more aware next time.

K: I know you mean well, but . . .

T: Come on now, Kathy, let's not make a major issue out of this. Let's forget it and enjoy ourselves now.

K *(becoming increasingly angry)*: I'm not finished discussing this yet. I have some more to . . .

T: All right, what do you want from me? What's it going to take from me to square things for me?

K: Now I'm really angry. You could begin by letting me finish one sentence for a change. You always interrupt me. That's what I mean by your not seeing me as a . . .

T: Now, don't get upset. I'm sorry. You're right. Say what you want to say.

K *(groaning slightly in exasperation)*: You see, you just did it again: you didn't let me finish my sentence again.

T: I'm sorry. Go ahead. Say what you want to say. I'll wait till you've finished.

N & T Evaluation:

> *Tim is obviously being toxic by interrupting when Kathy is speaking. Kathy is being self-poisoning primarily in two ways. First, she persistently tries to express herself to someone when it is obvious that he is not going to allow her to express herself. Kathy also poisons herself by refusing to confront herself with her dilemma. ("What do I want to do when I am aware that Tim habitually interrupts me when I talk and never lets me finish expressing myself?")*

There was once an old woman shopping in a country market that abounded in produce of various kinds. There was one stall after another, each offering the same varieties of fruits and vegetables, each with an eager hawker promising that his selection was the very finest. The old woman obviously knew what she was doing. She passed some stalls without a glance. She stopped at others momentarily. Still others she scrutinized carefully, usually focusing on a particular fruit or vegetable while ignoring the rest of the produce at this particular stall. Her final selection was carefully hand-picked and made with knowing experience. She seemed to have an almost intuitive sense, with which she chose the best available and avoided the inferior items.

The woman shopping in the market is analogous to each of us searching for satisfying human relationships. We face the same problem of selection. Like the old woman selecting her produce, we too need to be aware of the variety of relationships available to fulfill our need for nourishing relationships.

Relationships can nourish us and provide joyful, happy experiences, or they can be toxic and destructive, leaving us deprived and frustrated. We can learn only from our own experience how to discriminate between relationships which are nourishing, healthy, and gratifying and those which are frustrating and will tend to make us ill. Our awareness of how we experience our interaction with others provides us with the raw data from which to recognize and reach out for nourishing relationships and, equally important, to minimize those which are ungratifying and toxic. We experience some individuals as attractive, alive, vital, and exciting; they are the potentially nourishing, gratifying human beings. They have more to give us in a relationship when they choose to do so. There are others who have an air of unhealthiness or deadness about them, and we experience them as being dull, uninteresting, or even repulsive. They have less to give us in a relationship and tend to sap the vitality from those of us who encounter them.

Like any process involving human growth, the ability to be discriminating in one's relationships is an ongoing learning process. It involves our commitment to take responsibility for the kind of relationships in which we involve ourself. Discovering and discriminating between nourishing and toxic relationships begins with an attitude of openness to human encounters and an awareness of how we experience each interaction.

The human organism provides itself with a wealth of experiential data which it utilizes to one degree or another for its survival and growth. For us to utilize this marvelous human capability, it is essential that we be aware of *what* we do in this continuous process and *how* we do it. These capabilities function most effectively when we are not doing too much to distort and block our natural functioning. These potentials for emotional well-being and creativity develop naturally when they are not excessively hampered or distorted by toxic encounters and experiences. Toxic patterns have their origins in past experiences, beginning with childhood, and may continue to operate indefinitely, to the detriment of the individual. They always operate to some degree in everyone. The process of emotional nourishment involves awareness of *what* distortions and blocks are occurring and *how* they operate destructively to hamper our capabilities.

The self-poisoning patterns described in the preceding chapter will also invariably be manifested in the way in which the self-poisoner relates to others. What he does to himself—*i.e.*, *what* particular self-poisoning patterns he has adopted—he will also do to others, although rarely with the same tenacity and intensity. How a person poisons himself and how he poisons others are essentially two sides of the same coin. His self-poisoning pattern is often a private matter about which he remains silent and unsharing. With other people, he usually hides his fears about how others would react to him were he to express himself more openly.

Because the self-poisoner is a more suppressed person, he is handicapped in his ability to relate to others in a meaningful, intimate, open fashion. When he does become involved and begins to feel more secure about the relationship, his self-poisoning pattern is increasingly likely to appear in a similar toxic attitude directed against the other. Thus, the person who poisons himself by criticizing and finding fault with everything he does ("I'm never good enough") will become increasingly critical of the other person as he becomes more secure and comfortable in the relationship. This usually means that the other person has been poisoned and a pattern of toxic relating has evolved.

Toxic relating always requires the cooperation of both people.

Because two people are always involved, the patterns of toxic relating are frequently referred to as "games." In fact, there are rules with which each person decides to play a toxic game. When one person quits, the game is over; one person cannot play it alone.

Johnny was three years old when he discovered that he could turn himself blue by holding his breath and that this drove his mother into an absolute panic, so that she would do anything to get him to stop. Johnny quickly learned to blackmail his mother by holding his breath until she gave in to his demands. Their relationship became more and more toxic as he pushed his mother further and further. Filled with anxiety and resentment, she became less loving and more intent on discovering countermanipulations to prevent Johnny from holding his breath. After professional consultation, she became aware of Johnny's "game" and (being reassured by her physician that his breath-holding was harmless) decided not to play any more. As soon as she allowed him to

hold his breath as long as he wanted, the game
was over, and he gave it up.

**A person traps himself when he attempts to get
the other person to stop playing his game. This
usually only leads to different toxic games. An
effective antidote depends on the person's discovering how *he* perpetuates toxic interaction by
continuing to play his part.**

A human relationship is invariably a one-to-one
interaction. A person can no more relate to two people simultaneously than he can read two books at the
same time. However intimate a person may seem in
his simultaneous relating to more than one other person, this can never be anything more than a rapid
shifting back and forth of the focus of his attention
from one person to another. A charismatic personality
may captivate a large audience and hold them spell-
bound. Each of them is relating to him; he has their
full attention. He is not relating personally except as
he focuses his attention on one member of the audience. At best, he is apt to do this only momentarily.

The potential for nourishment in a relationship is
directly related to the degree of mutual emotional
involvement. A relationship becomes mutually nourishing as it increasingly meets the needs of both people. Intimacy evolves primarily through one-to-one
relating. It can be defined as a state of emotional
involvement between two people based on mutual
openness, trust, and caring.

Toxic relating can occur regardless of the degree of

intimacy. Toxic relating is characterized by a lack of respect and appreciation for the integrity and freedom of self-determination of another person. Instead, it is based on pressure, coercion, and intrusion for the purpose of getting the other person to do what the manipulator wants.

Manipulation is the hallmark of toxic relating.

Whether out of love or out of greed, the manipulator attempts to do something to the other person. Manipulation can be nourishing when the manipulator is open and clear about what he wants to do and what his purpose is *and* the other person is willing to be manipulated.

PATIENT: I have this tight feeling in my chest. It seems to come on at various times when I am under pressure. I feel like something wants to come out and I don't know what it is or how to get it out.

THERAPIST: I have something in mind, if you are willing to try an experiment.

PATIENT: What is it you want me to do?

THERAPIST: Would you be willing to scream into a pillow?

P: (*Feeling uneasy and with an embarrassed smile coming over his face*) I can't scream; I've never been able to. I think I'm afraid to scream.

T: Are you willing to take the risk and see what happens if you scream into a pillow?

P: Okay. I'll try it.

T: Hold the pillow over your face, as tightly or loosely as you want to, and scream as loud as you can. *(Patient puts the pillow over his face and several seconds later begins a series of short, muffled screams.)*

T: What are you experiencing now?

P: I feel myself holding back . . . I'm still afraid to really let loose.

T: I notice that you start to scream and abruptly cut your screaming off. Try it again, only this time let yourself scream as long as you can and be aware of when you cut yourself off.

P: Okay. I'll give it all I've got. *(Patient gives several loud, long screams into the pillow, gradually loosening the firmness with which he holds the pillow over his face.)*

P: Boy, *that* really felt good. I feel like I got something out that time.

T: Your face looks much more alive now, and I notice you're breathing more fully.

P: Yes, I'm aware of that too. I'm also aware of a lot of anger that came to me while I was screaming. *(The rest of the hour was spent exploring the patient's angry feelings and his awareness that his constricted feelings were related to his unexpressed anger and resentments.)*

In nourishing manipulation, a contract or agreement is openly stated and agreed upon by both people. An element of trust is involved, in that the manipulated person is willing to give his consent on the basis of his trust and confidence in the integrity of the other person.

Toxic relating is characterized by manipulations in which deception is the byword. Trust is sacrificed for the sake of expediency and achieving the desired results by whatever means are necessary.

The following dialogue took place between a mother and her six-year-old daughter, who had to undergo a tonsillectomy:

MOTHER: I want you to get dressed now. We have to go see the doctor today.

DAUGHTER: Why do I have to go see him again?

MOTHER: He just wants to look at you, dear. He's not going to hurt you. (*I'm going to be deceptive to accomplish my immediate purpose, and this is more important than the effects of my deception on our relationship.*)

DAUGHTER: That's what you told me last time, and he did hurt me.

M: That didn't really hurt. You were just scared. Now get dressed or we'll be late. (*I don't see you as a person. I won't accept your feelings as valid. I know how you feel better than you know how you feel.*)

(*The child begins to sob and dress slowly, while her mother brings out a suitcase she had previously packed for her daughter's stay in the hospital.*)

M: Are you ready to go?

D: (*Very reluctantly*) I guess so . . . What's that for? (*Pointing to the suitcase*)

M: That's just some old clothes I'm going to drop off later at the church. (*I'll get this job done any way I can, even by lying to you.*)

(*Mother and daughter drive to the hospital.*)

D: *(Getting quite panicky)* This isn't the doctor's office. This is a hospital.

M: Now, don't get excited. He's going to see you here today. *(More toxic deception)*

D: *(Crying hysterically now)* He's going to hurt me. What's he going to do to me? What's going to happen to me? Am I going to die?

M: Now, you're going to be all right. I'm going to stay with you. The doctor's decided that your tonsils have to come out, and I didn't want to tell you any sooner than I had to because I didn't want you to be upset any longer than necessary.

D: You lied to me! You tricked me! You told me he wasn't going to hurt me—he just wanted to look at me.

M: I told you I didn't want you to be upset and crying all the way to the hospital. If I had told you yesterday, you would have cried all day and made a big fuss. Now you're here and it will soon be over with.

Undoubtedly, this mother acted with good intentions, believing that she could spare her daughter and herself more anxiety and pain by her deception. The toxic manipulation—even when done out of love—of this kind of episode occurs in the message that Mother's word can no longer be trusted. The mother accomplished her goal—a minimal time of anxiety for her daughter—but the way she did it damaged the trust, openness, and intimacy of their relationship.

A more nourishing way for the mother to relate to her daughter would be as follows:

MOTHER: You know all the sore throats and colds you've been having? Well, the doctor believes that your tonsils are causing the trouble, and he wants to take them out. In that way he thinks you won't get sick so often.

DAUGHTER: *(Becoming upset and beginning to cry)* I don't want my tonsils out. I'll be more careful to wear sweaters when I go outside. I won't get sick any more. You'll see.

MOTHER: I was unhappy to hear that the doctor wants to take your tonsils out. I asked him if there was anything else we could do, and he felt it would only be postponing the matter and you would keep getting more infections.

DAUGHTER: *(Still upset and crying)* Do I have to? Can't we just wait another week or so? Is it going to hurt?

M: The doctor wouldn't do this if he didn't believe it was necessary and postponing it would probably make you worry more. They put you to sleep for a little while so you won't even know when your tonsils are being taken out. The doctor said you might have a sore throat for a few days.

D: What's the suitcase for?

M: We're going to the hospital to have it done, and these are some things you'll need while you're there.

D: Are you going to stay with me?

M: Yes. I'll be with you all the time until the operation, and I'll be there when you wake up.

Pain is an inevitable part of life, and the best the mother can do is to be honest with her daughter. By being honest with her daughter, the mother shares this unpleasant experience, respecting her daughter's fears and anxieties and doing all she can to provide security and comfort. In this way she helps her daughter to accept the unpleasant experience that she is to undergo.

Reality exists only in the present. Reality for each person involves what is actually occurring within himself and in his interacting with his environment at any given moment. Awareness of reality involves awareness of the experiential data from the five senses as well as countless body feelings and sensations. Full awareness involves "messages" which we receive from all these various sources of sensory data. This kind of "listening" means being "tuned in" to *oneself*: that is, consciously experiencing these data with full, clear, undistorted reception. Although there are some distortions, the body continuously and persistently states what it needs and what it doesn't need. The awareness-reaction-expression process is relentless. The continuing issue is always whether the person is interested in listening and reacting.

From the first time Burt met Linda, he was extremely attracted to her. Linda was quiet; she rarely had much to say, and her conversations with Burt were usually limited to responding to him. He decided on all their activities and how they would spend their time together. He was quite willing to take this role, and Linda seemed comfortable following his lead and usually went along with whatever he suggested.

Their involvement grew, and both stopped dating other people. Burt frequently had vague feelings that "She's just too good to be true." Linda never seemed irritated or angry with him. Apparently there was nothing she didn't like about him. He gave her a great deal of attention—took her to various interesting places and spent a good deal of his time with her. He would buy her gifts, which she always seemed to like and appreciate.

Gradually, he became uncomfortable in his role as the "sole director" of their relationship. He asked her more frequently to tell him what *she* would like to do or make some suggestions on her own about what activity they should share or place they should visit. She continued her pleasant, compliant manner and smilingly insisted that it didn't matter; whatever he wanted was fine. As their relationship continued, her attitude became increasingly irritating to Burt. He was frankly bewildered by his own attitude and decided that it was his hang-up that caused him to be anxious over such a "good thing."

Shortly after their engagement, Burt's company won a large government contract which required him to work overtime several evenings a week and occasionally on Saturday. When he was late or felt too tired to do anything and wanted to go to bed, Linda became sullen and quietly irritated. When he returned at nine or ten o'clock in the evening, he would often call to tell her he was too tired to come over. She continued her compliant attitude, but would sigh quietly into the phone when these instances occurred. When he asked her why she sighed, Linda would respond, "Oh, nothing." And they would hang up. Burt felt irritated at her sulking and at the same time guilty that he wasn't meeting her needs. He tried to explain to her that he had no choice and that the temporary extra work he was doing could mean a great deal to their future. Linda seemed totally uninterested in these bright possibilities for their future.

Somehow, they managed to weather their difficulties. The overtime ended, and shortly thereafter they were married. Burt was an energetic man who enjoyed varied activities and had a great many friends. He wanted to share these with Linda. He was usually much sought after at social gatherings, while Linda quietly stayed by his side, saying very little and rarely initiating contact with other people on her own. It became clear to Burt that when she sighed something was wrong, although usually when he inquired, he received a curt answer, "Oh, nothing."

Linda became less affectionate, less sexually responsive, and more withdrawn. Burt began to resent this, and gradually their difficulties reached a crisis in a rather violent argument in which Linda accused Burt of not loving her any more. He had been so solicitous and attentive before they were married, and now he was neglecting her. He reassured her of his love and tried to explain that he had other needs and commitments. Finally, she revealed her hidden attitude which had been there all along: "If you loved me, you would *always* put me first above everything else. If your job is more important than me, I don't see how you can really mean it when you say you love me."

The subtle cues of Linda's helpless, dependent attitude were there from the beginning, if Burt had been willing to explore them more fully. Linda was satisfied and compliant as long as the excitement and passion of their new romance was such that both longed to be together every moment possible. After their marriage, when the commitments, other interests, and needs of Burt's over-all life style began to emerge more fully, Linda's resentment and her clinging attitude became obvious.

Since everyone manifests both nourishing and toxic behavior patterns, the labeling of people as N or T is for descriptive purposes. In any relationship, there are always the questions, What is each person in the relationship doing that is nourishing and toxic? How do they nourish each other and how do they poison each other? These nourishing and toxic patterns are part of the dynamic process of the relationship and change as the relationship evolves. Two people may initially seem to be overwhelmingly nourishing to each other. Just as a love relationship usually has a preponderance of nourishing interaction, so the deterioration of a relationship is marked by increasing toxicity. Toxic relating is heavily loaded with games of rivalry, entrapment, deception, and other forms of falseness and manipulation. In each instance, the poisoner is seeking illegitimate satisfaction from the other person—that is, gratification of needs that the other is not willing to give. The victim feels increasingly drained, burdened, or resentful about the relationship. The manifestations of an increasingly toxic relationship are also apparent in the futile conflicts that develop in a deteriorating relationship. As the relationship draws to a close, the toxicity is frequently expressed in increasingly intense bitterness, resentment, and anger which all but obscure the previously nourishing love relationship. One or both are filled with poison and may wonder what they ever saw in the other.

Ellen and William Brewster had known each other since they were twelve. William's family had been socially prominent for three generations. His great-uncle had been mayor of the town, and the family were pillars of the community. Ellen's family were original settlers of the area, and one of the principal streets bore the family name. Since Ellen and William had gone steady through high school and college, their marriage was an event everyone had expected. William was a partner in the family law firm, while Ellen had master's degrees in both anthropology and archaeology and was pursuing her avid interest in the cultural patterns and mores of American Indian tribes. She had already made significant research contributions in her field and had several publications to her name.

The Brewsters' marriage was blissful for three years while they shared much together and also continued following their own professions and separate interests. They were both busy people, happily married and enjoying life. A year later, their first child was born, and their joy was even greater. A second and a third child followed, three years apart. Ellen willingly gave up her professional activities and enjoyed her role as mother and housewife, at the same time developing an increasingly active role in community affairs. To their family and friends, the Brewsters were an example of a really good marriage.

Their first major disagreement arose when, after their youngest child entered school, Ellen again wanted to pursue her professional activities. She was thirty-eight years old and had been offered a teaching position at a local college. She explained to William that she was becoming bored working on fund-raising committees and in other organizational activities. They always enjoyed a live-in maid, who had been with them since the birth of their second child and was like one of the family. Ellen was emphatic about having no intention of neglecting her children, but admitted that if she accepted a position at the college, she would not arrive home until close to dinner time three days each week.

To Ellen's surprise, William was adamant in his objection to her wishes. He insisted that "It was fine for you to do what you wanted when we didn't have a family, but now you have a full-time job in the home. Perhaps when the children are older we'll talk about it again." Ellen was startled at her husband's reaction and his unrelenting attitude. They quarreled bitterly over the issue. The stronger her stand, the more he insisted that he was the head of the house and the final decision was his. Each time she tried to discuss it calmly, they ended in a bitter argument.

Ellen turned down the offer to teach and continued her usual activities. Over the next few years, she gradually became withdrawn, seemed to lack energy, and began complaining of various

physical symptoms. William had surged ahead
through the years in his career and was being
considered as a candidate for the state senate.
He was unaware that sharing his achievements
with his wife was meeting with less and less
enthusiasm from her. Her preoccupation was
increasing with her somatic complaints and insom-
nia. Her physician suggested she try sleeping
alone in a separate room—that perhaps she would
thus be able to sleep better, since William's sleep
was often fitful and his squirming would awaken
her. Without much reaction, he agreed. In desperation, Ellen thought of seeing a psychothera-
pist. She knew that William would scoff at this
idea and come up with his usual suggestion of
more social activities and organizational work.
She began to drink quietly—first at bedtime, and
gradually extending earlier into the day.

Ellen was in her early fifties when their last
child went away to college. One night she calmly
walked into William's study and told him that she
wanted a divorce. He couldn't have been more
surprised. Once he realized she wasn't joking, his
response was one of outrage as he accused her of
being selfish and inconsiderate. He suggested that
she was deliberately trying to wreck his career at
its peak. Without exception, both families rallied
to his cause. They accused Ellen of being spoiled
and unappreciative. How could she complain
when she had everything? There had never been
a divorce on either side of the family. "You could
at least consider what this would do to the children," they told her, and that was their final word
on the subject.

The pressure was too much for Ellen to stand up against. Her only opportunities now to return to her profession were to accept positions in other parts of the country where she would have to work her way back into her field more slowly. She simply did not have the strength and determination to give up her entire life and face the rejection of her whole family.

Emotionally, her relationship with William was clearly at an end. It is questionable whether he was concerned about or even aware of this. He had always considered his wife's interests along these lines as silly notions, and when she stopped talking about them, he simply assumed she had come to her senses again. For Ellen, life had become a dull routine in which she struggled only to pass the time with the least amount of boredom. Her marriage had long since become totally dead. She had never moved back into the bedroom with William—and he had never asked her to. Their friends, relatives, and families still pointed with pride and joy to William and Ellen as a shining example of a stable, enduring, blissful marriage.

When a person finds a relationship to be poisonous, he can reject the toxic intrusions by protecting himself or reacting against the other's poison. Or, he can counterattack and become more poisonous himself.

No one wants to be poisoned, and when a person seemingly allows this to happen, there is always some gratification. Toxic interaction often continues in a relationship because of a lack of awareness by either or both of the people involved. The patterns described on the following pages focus on attitudes and behavior that are obviously destructive to intimacy. Involving oneself in a poisonous relationship also invariably reflects a self-induced toxic pattern.

Toxic interaction is marked by the absence of direct contact and confrontation between two people.

When two people who have shared a healthy relationship stop relating honestly, defensive walls grow and are manifested in the way they contact each other. While the game is never verbalized, they have a tactical rule that, for example, each looks at the other only when the other is not looking first. By taking turns looking at each other, they avoid eye contact and can more easily conceal themselves from each other. There is no honest attempt to resolve the real conflicts or alleviate the poisonous interaction. The relationship becomes increasingly toxic. This is in contrast to the enjoyment and nourishment two loving, caring people experience in looking at and touching each other.

Under the stress of frustration, the T person typically attempts to resolve his conflict by changing other people rather than by using his resources to experiment and discover potential solutions from within himself. Each individual has his patterns of toxic manipulation—his personal repertoire of "numbers" with which to control other people. His most prominent "numbers" are those behavior patterns which he has found most effective. In each instance, when his manipulations succeed, his gratification is at the expense of the person he has manipulated. One way or another, the T person exploits his victim. In intimate relating, each manipulative endeavor has a toxic effect which is disruptive to the development and continuation of intimacy.

Toxic manipulation is exemplified by the following dialogue which took place between a husband and wife after she decided to invite her mother to visit for a week.

MRS. BROWN: Dear, Mother called today. She seems lonely and depressed and did everything but ask outright if she could come for a visit.

MR. BROWN: You know how I feel about her. Every time she comes, she sticks her nose in our business and you and I end up fighting.

MRS. BROWN: Well, I really didn't know how to get out of it . . . I don't want to hurt her feelings or make her feel unwanted.

MR. BROWN: You mean she's already coming? Is that what you're telling me?

MRS. B: Well, what else could I tell her? I can't tell her that her own daughter doesn't want to see her even for a week.

MR. B: You could at least tell her that you would talk it over with me and let her know.

MRS. B: She knows you don't like her, and I was afraid that would just make her anxious.

MR. B: (*Sarcastically*) Well, we can't make your dear old mother anxious, even if it does annoy me and create problems between us.

MRS. B: (*Preparing the hook for one of her best numbers*) Please, sweetheart, do this for me and you won't be sorry . . . I'll make it up to you. (*Mrs. Brown sits down by her husband, puts her arm around him, and kisses him on the ear.*)

MR. B: *(Somewhat irritated)* What do I have to do, buy your affection? I feel like you're bribing me, and you haven't been very warm toward my advances lately.

MRS. B: I know, but if you do this for me, I'll make it up to you. You'll see. You won't be sorry.

MR. B: Now, exactly how long does she plan to stay?

Seductiveness can, of course, be an honest, nourishing way of relating. In this instance, the wife uses it to manipulate her husband into going along with something she wants. Her seductiveness has a "hook" in it. In essence, they make a deal in which each gets "paid off" for giving the other what he wants.

A degree of manipulation is present in any kind of agreement that is not spontaneously or willingly accepted by each person. Manipulative interaction always involves some degree of deception. Mrs. Brown has discovered that her "seductive number" works when she wants something from her husband that he is unwilling to give. In this case, he will probably *act* pleasant toward his mother-in-law. In so doing, he decides to play a game of his own. Since he is poisoning himself in this way, his dishonesty in turn will most likely lead to resentment toward his wife, his mother-in-law, or himself, and a new toxic encounter is in the making. A cycle of poisonous interaction may continue indefinitely in this way. It may appear as only a series of unconnected episodes, but in reality it is a process of ongoing toxic relating.

Nourishing manipulation (an open, honest contract) in the same circumstance is illustrated in the following dialogue.

Mrs. Brown: Dear, I would like to invite Mother to stay with us for a week.

Mr. Brown: I don't enjoy your mother's visits. She disrupts our household with her criticisms, and in the past you and I have had some bitter fights because of her presence. I resent her staying with us.

Mrs. Brown: I know how you feel. I feel a conflict about her visits too. You are the most important person in the world to me *and* I do like to invite Mother out once every year or so. She's getting old, and I know she's lonely, and it means a lot to her. I feel I'm giving her something very important for her at this time in her life. I don't particularly enjoy spending a great deal of time with her, but I do feel a certain commitment to give what I can to make her life a little more meaningful.

Mr. Brown: How long do you want to invite her for?

Mrs. B: I'd like to invite her for about ten days.

Mr. B: I know how you feel about your mother, so I'm willing to go along with your invitation. I do wish that she was only going to be here a week, though.

Mrs. B: Thank you. I plan to invite some of my girl friends and their mothers to lunch, and maybe Mother will receive some invitations to spend some time with them while she is visiting with us.

A nourishing relationship involves compromise. Each person never wholly has his way. The critical

aspect illustrated in the above dialogue is the direct,
honest statement of the situation (Mrs. Brown wants
her mother to visit, rather than playing the deceptive
game that her mother wants to come and Mrs. Brown
doesn't know how to get out of it). Mr. and Mrs.
Brown are open and straight in telling each other
how they feel about the situation. Mr. Brown decides
that he is willing (he doesn't have to want it) to go
along with his wife's request. She, in turn, directly asks
him for what she wants and leaves it to him to decide
whether he is willing or not. She does not play any
game of enticement or deception or offer some kind
of a "deal" to pay him back.

OWNING ONE'S INHIBITIONS

A person who feels a lack of nourishment may
attribute his frustration to the unreasonable refusal of
others to give him what he needs. A common attitude
exists that one has a right to expect nourishment from
another, as if it were owed to him. This attitude is
poisonous, whether the person openly demands what
he wants or has an additional expectation that the
other person should know what he needs and he
should not even have to ask for it.

A major ingredient in toxic relating is expressed in
the following statement: "If you really loved me,
you'd understand what I want and give it without my
asking." The poisoner is unwilling to openly ask for
what he wants from the other, is unwilling to accept
the responsibility for not being clear and direct, and in
addition, avoids his anxiety and inhibition by dumping the responsibility on the other. When he is success-

ful in putting this responsibility on the other person, the latter then becomes the one to blame. The manipulator uses his deceptive tactics to avoid owning (taking responsibility for) his phobia about rejection or, if burdened with deep feelings of being worthless and undeserving, his guilt and anxiety about asking for what he needs. The game becomes doubly poisonous when the victim is convinced that he should be able to meet the other's expectations. Both agree to play a toxic game in which the manipulator dumps his inhibitions on his victim, who then begins a self-poisoning pattern of apologizing and trying to do better. Somehow, he is never quite successful. The only way one person can consistently meet the expectations of another would be to be that person—or be clairvoyant. The stage is set for an ongoing, chronic pattern of toxic relating in which both people are continually frustrated as they play out their toxic game.

Toxic people strongly resist acknowledging their anxieties and inhibitions. Instead, they dump their difficulties on the other. They are unwilling to take the risk of sharing their problems, so that the other person is aware of what is really happening in the relationship. After all, once a person is willing to admit to his inhibitions and fears, the game is over, since he can no longer continue his deceptions. While this may seem the obvious thing to do, it fills the T person with anxiety. If he exposes his game, he has also confronted himself with seeking his own solution. He must now ask for what he wants and learn to tolerate rejections rather than accuse someone else of letting him down. This is about the last thing a T person is willing to attempt.

"SHOULD-ING"

"Should-ing" is a finger-pointing attitude in which one person asserts that he knows better how the other person *should* be, how he *should* act, and even how he *should* think or feel. It is a statement to another person that his self-determining capabilities are inadequate or in some way defective. Furthermore, the finger-pointer insists that his own way is superior.

Legitimately, "shoulds" are the voices of external authority which have the power to tell other people what to do. Such shoulds range from conforming to traffic laws to the moral shoulds of one's religious convictions. When a person lives within a group, he must necessarily submit to some forms of authority or else risk alienation, isolation, or punishment by the group. He *cannot* always be self-determining and still function within society.

In intimate relating, however, all shoulds are poison. Shoulds always imply an attempt at dominance and control by one person and a demand for submissiveness or compliance by the other.

Any struggle for control in a relationship is toxic to intimacy.

Shoulds also imply to the victim that he ought to be different—that in some way he is inadequate. In an ongoing relationship, this establishes an atmosphere of pressure and coercion in which the victim may feel he is being continually judged and evaluated. It encourages him to deliberately watch himself—what he says and what he does. It consequently inhibits the expression of his spontaneous self. The victim may habitually check out silently most of what he will say and do lest he put his foot in his mouth and be reprimanded for having violated some should. The best that the victim can do in his relating is avoid breaking any rules. The most he can hope for in this kind of relationship—if he is good enough—is to avoid criticism and to achieve approval and a pat on the back from the other.

When his well-being is in the hands of the powerful "should-er," poisonous interaction inevitably ensues. The victim may play "good boy" and seemingly want to please his tyrannical partner, but one way or another, knowingly or not, he will somehow undermine the whole program. When a person is dominated and oppressed, his resentment always festers until it finds some kind of expression. Usually, in should-ing games, the victim becomes a skillful saboteur and somehow always manages to undercut what the other wants from him, despite his "best intentions" to cooperate and please.

For example, all ideals reflect an attitude of how one *should* be. An ideal usually expresses the expectations of someone else (*e.g.*, a parent) which the person has accepted as valid. Such ideals are particularly venomous when the individual believes that his worth as a person rests on achieving them. They are typically excessively demanding.

SHOULD-ER (father): Well Bob, how did you do on your math final?

VICTIM (son): I did much better. I pulled a high B, and the prof said I'd probably get a B out of the course instead of a C.

SHOULD-ER: I knew you could do it. You should have buckled down earlier and you would've probably pulled an A.

VICTIM: Gee, Dad, for a while it was a sweat whether I would have to drop the course or risk flunking it. I thought you'd be pleased with me.

S: Well, I am pleased. I'm glad you didn't flunk. But you shouldn't get complacent just because you got a B. Remember, there's next semester to think about. You should start right in at the beginning working as hard as you can. Don't you agree, son?

V: Yeah, I guess you're right, Dad. It's just that sometimes I wish you would be satisfied . . . as if I'd done something well enough.

S: That's how you get complacent—and lazy. I believe no matter how well you do, you should always try harder to do better. That's how you really become a success.

THE BLAMING GAME

Blaming is not only a waste of energy, but a way of poisoning oneself and avoiding living in the present by holding to past experiences which cannot be undone. Blaming games are particularly tantalizing to those interested in maintaining power over others. When the other person errs, the blamer has irrefutable evidence with which to nail his victim to the cross. Toxic adults seek to lay their every unhappiness at the doorstep of their parents, who didn't understand them, or give them enough love, etc., even when they are aware that blaming their parents is a completely futile game which only serves as an excuse to rationalize away their own failings as self-determining adults.

Blaming implies that the other person "should have done better" in some way. The blamer is primarily interested in dumping his own feelings of guilt and shame on someone other than himself. His parents should not have "messed him up" so much; they should not have inhibited him so much; they should not have punished him so severely; they should have given him more love . . . etc. The supertoxic blamer even implies that his parents deliberately failed to give him what he needed as a child. The least the blamer could do in all fairness would be to blame his grandparents, since they were major factors in the development of the blamer's parents.

In any relationship, blaming is always a dead-end toxic game. In intimate relationships, it doesn't matter who is "right" or "wrong": when any variety of the blaming game persists, even the "winner" loses. The "winner" may feel self-righteous or self-satisfied about being one up. The "loser," who is stuck with the blame, usually wants to get even in some way with the "victor." Blaming another only nurtures a cycle of new, more intricate kinds of toxic relating.

NOURISHING AND TOXIC HUMOR

Humor generally carries with it a strong connotation of nourishing behavior. Humor and laughter are generally experienced as nourishing. The person feels lighthearted and joyous. His problems seem less ponderous and grim. He feels better about life.

Toxic forms of humor are recognizable by their detrimental effects. The most obvious kind of toxic humor occurs when a person is laughing *at* an individual rather than *with* him. A person who becomes the butt of a joke is left with feelings of humiliation, embarrassment, and rejection. The firecracker under the seat of an unknown victim lit by the sadistic practical joker is an obvious example of toxic humor. More subtle toxic humor is expressed by the person who watches others struggling to accomplish something and thoroughly enjoys their failures and mishaps. Meanwhile, he sits on the sideline and avoids taking any such risk himself.

THE "SNICKERER"

Some people poison the atmosphere by waiting until they can laugh or snicker at someone else's foibles, embarrassment, or difficulties. This poisonous attitude is observable in the gloating of the snickerer. He laughs at the expense of others. While he enjoys his humor, his victim is poisoned. Some people become embarrassed or inhibited when such a poisoner is present. Only a desperate person would attempt an ongoing intimate relationship with a snickerer. The snickerer takes particular delight in disrupting the joyful experience of another. Scarcely anything will take the joy out of an experience faster than to make the person self-conscious about his pleasure and excitement: "Boy, you sure are enjoying yourself; you sure are having a good time. I sure like to watch you laugh and have so much fun!" Often the victim is bewildered about what turns him off at this point. The poisoner, after all, has simply commented about something that would seem to be quite delightful. The poison is in the interruption itself and its effect of making the person self-conscious. Spontaneity and self-consciousness are antithetical.

DINGLEBERRY HUNTERS

Some people relate to others by focusing with a particularly critical eye on minute, trivial details (dingleberries) about the other's behavior, memory, knowledge, etc. They seem to be listening to what the other is sharing with them and appear genuinely interested. However, their responsiveness is top-heavy with interruptions or corrections whenever the other slips on slight details or makes trivial statements of misinformation. The dingleberry hunter in essence is an extremely pedantic "professional" corrector. Each time he discovers an error, he has another trophy for his collection. Sometimes he corrects slight grammatical flaws in the sentence structure of the other. Or, he may spot the tiniest piece of lint on his companion's clothing and carefully remove it with the skill of a neurosurgeon. He then smiles as if he had rendered a service. Continual exposure to this kind of "helpfulness" leaves one with a feeling of mild irritation which becomes poisonous by its constancy. The victim is further frustrated because each correction is so trivial that any real expression of resentment seems unwarranted. Obviously, the dingleberry hunter is a perfectionist—and, of course, insatiable. The victim can be reasonably assured that the dingleberry hunter will never be satisfied.

THE BULLY

The bully seems to exist for the purpose of demonstrating his ability to defeat other human beings at every opportunity. He uses his power for conquest and to make others feel fearful and intimidated. Ultimately, the bully is overwhelmed by his own strength, and in the end he poisons himself. As he struts about with a gloating, arrogant attitude, he loses the softness and sensitivity that could make him open to the nourishment from others which he desperately needs. The self-poisoning aspect of this pattern is manifested in his increasingly desperate bullying behavior as his frustration grows. He invariably avoids a fair fight and chooses opponents who are no match for him. He fights only battles in which he is clearly capable of overpowering his victim. The most obvious method is superior size and strength—as, for example, older siblings who beat up on their younger brothers or sisters, or parents who "bravely" challenge their children to move out if they feel dissatisfied. Other bullies are more subtle. Some bully with financial power—the department store buyer, for example, who teases or insults the hapless salesman.

Behind each bully is a frightened little person who inwardly, however vaguely, knows he is poison and unable to nourish anyone—even himself.

Antidote: Confronting oneself with the obvious. What do I want from this person? What do I hope to get for myself by continuing in a relationship in which I feel bullied and victimized? Do my answers to these questions seem sensible to me?

PEOPLE EATERS

One of the most toxic behavior patterns appears in the person who psychologically devours other people.

He practices a kind of psychic cannibalism. He often appears to be a well-adjusted, capable, self-reliant, giving, nourishing person. It is only after the victim has invested considerable energy and is emotionally involved that he discovers what is happening to him. The poison from the "people eater" may appear suddenly in a huge dose, or the victim may experience it in the form of chronic pain and frustration. In the first instance, the victim has an acute experience of being poisoned, and the relationship comes to an abrupt end. He feels as if the carpet had been pulled out from under him, and he may be dazed and bewildered about what happened and how he could have been so wrong about the other person. Invariably, he feels used, exploited, and drained. In chronic form, the victim is bled white, after which the poisoner resumes his nourishing façade and maintains it until his victim is reassured.

An example is the parent who feeds on his child throughout the years the child is growing to adulthood—even longer if the opportunity exists. A mother may appear loving and interested in helping her son become a healthy, happy, creative person. The poison first comes as a constant urging of the child to achieve, and when the child is successful in meeting her expectations, she grabs—sometimes literally grabs—the achievement away from him. When, for example, the child comes home with an outstanding report card and greets his mother in the kitchen with his triumph, she takes one look at the report card and, without a word to her son, rushes into the living room to show the women in her bridge club what he has done. The child is ignored while his mother triumphs and basks in what should have been his glory, and his achieve-

ment is eradicated by the response of his mother. It is,
again, a form of psychological rape against his integrity as a person. Later, she may praise him and tell
him how proud she is, but the whole flavor of her
attitude is not appreciation of him for himself, but her
own personal triumph. It is as if he were not so much
her son as her chattel.

Another form of psychic cannibalism is that of the
classic con artist. In order to snare people, con artists
have to be charming and appealing in appearance
and manner. Such people have little or no human
compassion. They are very good at acting emotional,
but in reality they lack normal feelings and emotions.
Even sexually, they experience very little, although
their performance may be quite satisfying to their
partners. Sex is simply another way of holding their
victims captive. The cannibal is characterized by this
total lack of caring for his victim, who remains only
an object to be used for his satisfactions and subsequently discarded.

T people often come in very attractive, enticing
packages. They may have developed their manipulative pattern by discovering (usually in childhood)
that they have some appealing quality which draws
people to them and that they are able to manipulate
others with their special attraction.

Margaret was a vivacious, charming, outgoing
child who was found appealing by everyone. She
was the center of attention in her family. In her
teens, she was aware that all she needed to do
was act cute and "the boys came falling at my
feet." Her difficulties began in her early twenties
when she discovered that her conquests and her

ability to get people to do her bidding were becoming boring.

Chronic manipulators often discover at some point in their lives that they have no idea who they are. This discovery can produce sheer panic —particularly at the prospect of giving up their manipulative games. They sincerely believe that to be left to their own resources and called upon to stand on their own two feet would leave them alone and empty forever.

CONCLUSION

Sincerity and action in good faith can be met with manipulation and action in bad faith. In the practicalities of everyday relationships, the crucial issue of learning to be discriminating involves increasing awareness and efficiency of action in protecting oneself from the pitfalls of toxic relating. *Avoiding what is toxic or nonnourishing is the critical process that enables the person to experience emotionally nourishing relationships.*

The person who gives or loves indiscriminately contributes to his own destruction. In giving to a T person, one plants seeds in a barren field. The least one can do is be aware of the nature of the relationship. If a person, for his own reasons—ethical, moral, or other—continues to give to a T person, let him at least not delude himself that he will be nourished in return. When one acts out of a sense of duty or loyalty, he then makes his choice knowingly, and is therefore less likely to be frustrated.

When he feels no moral or ethical responsibility, the healthy, aware person will reconcile himself to some pattern of self-protection, reduced emotional investment, or outright termination of toxic relationships. The unaware or neurotic person, in contrast, remains stuck—unable to extricate himself. His strength is drained and not replenished, and he himself becomes increasingly toxic. Such people become bitter and cynical as this exhausting process continues. They may abandon their quest for meaningful human interaction, or they may seek to compensate for their emptiness with distractions or substitutes: for example, the compulsive businessman, the alcoholic, and the recluse.

A human being's existence is a process of interaction with his environment, from which he must continually seek nourishment. Many of his emotional needs can be legitimately satisfied only through nourishing relationships with others.

Nourishing relationships naturally evolve between people who are attracted to or interested in each other and who have not been poisoned excessively by earlier toxic experiences. Toxic relationships are unnatural in that they distort the way a person normally obtains nourishment from others. Man is not a creature who innately preys on his fellow man for the satisfaction of his needs. When toxic experiences have not been excessive, mutually nourishing ways of relating will spontaneously evolve.

CHAPTER SEVEN

Antidotes to Toxic Relating

INTRODUCTION

Nourishment in human relationships is an ongoing process. Consider a farmer with his orchard: The more care he gives it, the more fruit it is likely to give in return. However, when he plants his seed in barren soil, he may "give" until he is exhausted and starve to death in the process. It is the responsibility of each of us to discover when we are involved in a barren relationship.

The following series of questions compares attitudes and behavior patterns that are toxic to a relationship with those reflecting a more nourishing approach. These comparative questions are intended to sharpen the reader's awareness of his own way of interacting with others. In intimate relating, the *attitude* of the person is often more important than his actual behavior in yielding an understanding of his nourishing and toxic patterns.

T: Do I believe that the way other people relate to me should live up to my expectations—particularly when they are reasonable?

or

N: Do I believe that it is their right to relate to me as they choose?

T: Do I believe that, as a mature person, I must be my authentic self, openly and honestly expressing my feelings and point of view with everyone?

or

N: Do I believe that openness and honesty can at times be destructive to my own well-being or that of others?

T: As a loving, caring person do I believe that giving to someone should always provide me with some satisfaction?

or

N: Do I feel that I can poison myself by giving indiscriminately?

T: Do I push my givingness regardless of the other's responsiveness or lack of it?

or

N: When I give to another, do I make my offer with an open hand?

T: Do I believe that my judgment is superior to another's and that he can learn from my mistakes?

or

N: Do I believe that each person must discover for himself what is best for him?

T: Do I automatically move away from people who have shortcomings and "hang-ups"?

or

N: Do I accept the fact that everyone has some shortcomings?

T: Is my well-being primarily based on the approval of others?

or

N: Do my security and self-esteem stem primarily from within myself?

T: Do I allow others to manipulate me for fear of rejection if I do not comply with their demands?

or

N: Am I willing to say "no" when I feel manipulated and take my chances that the others will accept me anyhow?

T: Do I feel that anger and resentments are destructive to an intimate relationship?

or

N: Do I accept my anger and resentments as inevitable aspects of any intimate relationship?

T: Do I give largely out of feelings of obligation, duty, and guilt?

or

N: Is my giving motivated by my personal wanting and/or willingness to give?

T: Are my intimate relationships often a one-way street in which I give in the hope that eventually the other person will become giving toward me?

or

N: In my intimate relationships, do I also feel cared for and given to by the other person?

T: Does my giving have a "hook," in that I expect reciprocation?

or

N: Do I give primarily out of a need to express my caring toward another by giving?

T: Do I constantly "sell" my point of view, trying to get other people to agree with me?

or

N: Do I say what *I* want, need, resent, etc., and *feel* finished when I have completed my statement?

T: Am I usually on my own trip, ignoring the reactions of others (boredom, restlessness, irritation, etc)?

or

N: Do I feel in touch with the other people and
aware of their reactions?

T: Am I using others as a "dumping ground" to
release my pent-up frustrations and problems?

or

N: Am I genuinely interested in two-way com-
municating?

T: When someone is giving toward me, do I feel
indebted, as if I owed him something in return?

or

N: When someone gives to me, do I appreciate his
givingness and consider this a completed act?

T: Do I feel awkward, guilt-ridden, or otherwise
uncomfortable when others give to me?

or

N: Do I enjoy the givingness of others as an expression of their feeling toward me?

T: When someone speaks to me, am I simply
waiting for him to finish so that I can say what I
want to say?

or

N: When another person is talking to me, do I really
pay attention and listen to what he is saying?

T: Is the satisfaction of my self-expression based on
the other person's acceptance of (agreement
with) what I've just said?

or

N: Do I express myself to another person *primarily*
for my own need to express myself?

Although human relating is a major source of emotional nourishment, it is a mistake to believe that our well-being rests *primarily* on our relationships with others. Most T people sincerely believe that if only they could learn to "relate successfully," the bulk of their frustrations would be resolved. They project their own self-nourishing potentials onto others. They use their power to manipulate others into giving them what they want rather than to discover how to get what they need more legitimately (honestly). In toxic relationships, this attitude is combined with an expectation that each person has something coming from the other—that in various ways, they *owe* each other nourishment. In intimate relationships, this attitude sets the stage for countless forms of toxic interaction.

The simple fact of life is that each of us, if we are to survive, *must* depend on our own resources. When we fail to do this, when we become manipulative and nourish ourselves from others, we cannot manipulate them into giving us what we need without poisoning the relationship in the process.

The prime source of nourishing interaction is authentic, *intimate* relating. Genuine relating *is* responding to the other and to his needs.

Toxic attitudes in relating can be summarized as follows: "I would rather try to get someone else to give me what I need than to do the best I can to get it for myself." The person thereby assumes the "other-oriented" attitude of those who use their life energies in primarily toxic relationships, constantly trying to manipulate others.

The N person is not under the illusion that "maturity" means existing alone. His attitude is more open, honest, and authentic. When he is interested, he is willing to expend energy on (work at) developing a relationship and sustaining it. He does not have the fantasy that two people just come together and stay together spontaneously. His caring about his relationships is reflected in his awareness and concern about avoiding his own tendencies to be manipulative. At the same time, he protects himself from allowing the other person to relate to him in a toxic manner. He does this without becoming toxic himself (fighting poison with poison).

N people recognize that there is a necessary balance between self-nourishment and those needs satisfied through relationships with others. At the same time, they try to keep their interaction as positive and nourishing as possible.

TOXIC JOHN: Did you put gas in the car, like I asked you to?

NOURISHING MARY: No. I had intended to earlier, but Helen [John's sister] called. Her car broke down and had to be towed to a garage, and she asked me to pick her up and take her home. Then I was late for my dental appointment and had to rush to pick up the children at school.

TOXIC JOHN: I'd like to get this kind of thing settled once and for all. When I ask you to do something and you agree, I expect you to do it.

NOURISHING MARY: Most of the time I am able to do what you ask. Sometimes unexpected things come up and I can't.

T.J.: Every time it happens, you always have some

excuse. Either your mother dropped over, or one of the kids was sick, or there was a big line at the check-out stand at the market—always something.

N.M.: When I don't get something done, I feel you are entitled to know the reason why I didn't do it.

T.J.: I don't give a damn about your reasons; you're just getting too sloppy about meeting your obligations, and I think you ought to do something about it.

N.M.: I don't accept that, and I resent your general indictment. You make it sound like a breach-of-contract case.

T.J.: Even your mother says the same thing about you—she's always talking about what a sloppy room you had as a child.

N.M.: Any other junk you want to throw at me because I didn't put gas in the car?

T.J.: Since you brought it up, I've also been noticing that the house is getting rather sloppy. Maybe you should cut down on some of your club activities.

N.M.: I resent your generalizations every time we get into an argument. I wish you would stick to the point. I'm sorry I didn't get gas in the car.

T.J.: I'm not letting you off the hook that easy—I think it's time you became a more responsible person.

N.M.: I really resent your condescending attitude. I'm not going to continue to bicker with you.

T.J.: That's it. Cop out. You're never willing to settle anything.

N.M.: I'm not willing to play the bad one every time I don't meet your expectations.

T.J.: There you go, trying to get off the hook again. There's an important issue here, and I insist that we see it through and reach an agreement. I'm tired of being victimized by your negligence.

N.M.: I feel like I'm being nailed to the cross. I will not play the part of a criminal. I don't feel you're even interested in understanding, least of all appreciating, all the things I do accomplish each day.

T.J.: Yeah, yeah. I know—you lead a hard life.

N.M.: I give up. I'm leaving for my P.T.A. meeting. I have to introduce the speaker.

T.J.: What about my dinner?

N.M.: It's on the stove. *You* said you'd be home at six o'clock. We waited forty-five minutes for you, and the children and I ate. Otherwise, I'd be late for my meeting.

The N person is aware that everyone is toxic to some degree and that he will inevitably experience toxic interaction in the routine of daily living. He accepts this reality and is not instantaneously hostile toward the toxic behavior of others. He accepts the fact (recognizes) that their toxic patterns are part of their struggle to survive and get what they need and not really directed at himself. The nourishing person is not incensed by toxic people and does not criticize them as if they were "bad" or "evil" or "should" change. While he avoids allowing himself to be poisoned, he does not try to make the other person give up his toxic behavior.

Since toxic patterns exist in everyone, discovering

how to protect oneself from them is vital to living a nourishing life. The only other alternative is a constant fleeing from relationship to relationship and eventual isolation of the self. If one wishes to avoid eating poisonous food, starvation is scarcely the answer.

MARILYN: I've been kicked around since I was a kid. I'm thirty years old and I've had three marriages—all three men turned out to be bastards—and now I've got three children to support and be both mother and father to. I'm fed up. I want somebody to take care of *me* for a change. It's just not fair! Why can't I find a guy who loves me and wants to take care of me? What's wrong with me? There are plenty of girls who don't have half as much on the ball as I do and they seem to find nice husbands.

This common toxic attitude is based on the cultural myth that "the world is fair and justice always triumphs in the end." When one has suffered long enough, or had enough "bad breaks," eventually the scales will balance—the tables will turn, and the victim too will finally find happiness . . . just as he was promised as a little child.

While Marilyn wasn't this unrealistic, she did convey her expectations toward the men she met more than she realized. Silently, she observed them with a scrutinizing eye to see whether "he's just after my body or whether he's really interested in me (and taking care of me)."

When she met Gregg, things began to look brighter. She had periodically met men who

were attentive and caring and wanted a meaningful relationship. Most of them simply did not
interest her—they were too passive or not exciting
enough. Gregg was an exception. He immediately
took to Marilyn and also seemed to enjoy her
children. He liked being with them and they
with him. Being in an executive position with a
chain of retail stores, he passed her "financially
responsible" test. His sexual interest in Marilyn
was also very acceptable. Gregg was an appetizing man whose quiet availability and sensitivity
were very appealing to her. They were married
nine months after they met.

Gregg had two children by a former marriage.
His ex-wife had not remarried and had moved
back to her home town to live with her parents.
Marilyn knew that Gregg spent two to three
weeks each summer with his children. Gregg sent
his ex-wife monthly alimony checks without fail.
While he earned a good salary, these payments
did limit his spendable income. Nevertheless, they
bought a home and were able to live reasonably
well.

Gradually, the alimony checks began to grate
on Marilyn's nerves. She again began to feel
gypped. "I knew he was too good to be true," she
confided to a girl friend. "If it weren't for his
ex-wife, we could really live well." (She left out
Gregg's children altogether in her comment.)
"Why couldn't I find a guy who wasn't all snarled
up in alimony payments?"

Marilyn began to express her irritation about
this to Gregg. He tried to reassure her that the
future looked bright. He felt there were real

opportunities for advancement in his company, although none was immediately in sight. Blinded by her bitter "the world owes me a living" attitude, she failed to appreciate her relationship with Gregg, their feelings for each other, and the life style that he had been able to provide for her. She seemed to quickly forget her former two-bedroom apartment in a noisy building filled with "divorced women and screaming children." She persisted in her attitude that the world owed her more, that the ledgers were far from balanced. She expressed her bitterness by withdrawing. ("If I'm not getting what I want, why should I put out for anybody else?") She began neglecting the house, running up bills in department stores, and nagging Gregg about when he was going to be promoted. Gregg continued to be apologetic, and the poisonous aspects of the relationship grew.

Marilyn had wanted an active social life, and Gregg went along with her wishes in the hope that she would be more satisfied. Instead, she would comment about how successful the other men were—and they didn't have an ex-wife hanging on their coattails.

Marilyn was particularly attracted to the husband of one of the couples with whom they frequently socialized. She subtly let Bob know of her interest, having decided: "I've got a right to do what I need to be happy; I've got it coming. Why should I sacrifice myself? Look at all I've been through." Her girl friend reminded her how outspoken Gregg had always been against infidelity, but Marilyn simply said that she was sick and tired of being cheated and settling for so little. If people weren't going to give her what she had a right to, she was going to take it.

Marilyn began meeting Bob in the afternoons in out-of-the-way restaurants and motels. When Bob's wife began to get suspicious, he told Marilyn he was not going to see her any more—that he didn't want to jeopardize his marriage. Marilyn was outraged at Bob (another unfair blow). He agreed to continue to see her, although less often and under more cautious circumstances. This didn't really satisfy Marilyn; she felt she had a right to her affair and resented the restrictions. At parties, she made increasing insinuations that Bob was a "chaser." Gregg got angry and asked her why she was "being so bitchy."

One night when they came home from a party at which she had been particularly obnoxious, Gregg insisted that she "stop taking pot shots at Bob" or he wasn't going to attend any more parties. Marilyn blew up in anger and told Gregg that she *knew* Bob was having an affair. Gregg insisted that regardless of what Bob was doing, it was none of her business. The argument became increasingly heated until finally Marilyn told Gregg the truth.

Gregg was stunned. "I've tried to make you happy; I've put up with your constant complaining, and I hoped that you would somehow again be more loving toward me. I was willing to overlook anything, but this is too much. I'm leaving." As he walked out of the living room, Marilyn shouted a few choice phrases about all men being bastards. Gregg packed a suitcase and left the same night.

For Marilyn, the world had again dealt her a lousy hand. She instructed her attorney to take Gregg for everything he had. Since they had been married only three years, the judge awarded her the house and its furnishings and nothing else. Marilyn was again outraged, this time against the judge.

The attitude that the world is unfair stems directly from T people's reluctance to take responsibility for their own lives. They insist that external forces of some kind are somehow supposed to provide them with what they need—that somehow not only do they have a right to happiness, but this happiness should be provided by someone else. With this attitude, the person rarely stops to appreciate the needs of the next person, who is also interested in satisfying himself.

In a nourishing (nonmanipulative) relationship, nobody owes anybody anything.

This attitude is particularly meaningful when one is interested in intimate relating. Intimacy is best nourished in a free and open atmosphere in which neither person is interested in pressuring, controlling, or changing the other. Each states what he wants and what he doesn't want (resents). Each decides when and how he will respond to the needs of the other. When a person is honestly *asking* for something, he accepts the other's freedom to respond as he chooses, including ignoring his request entirely. Each person decides not only what he is willing to give, but also what his responsibilities, duties, and obligations are to the other. Each establishes his own code of behavior and takes responsibility for it. This prevailing attitude is clearly stated and accepted by both people. In a nourishing relationship, everything is made as explicit as possible.

IT TAKES TWO TO PLAY

A person is obviously more vulnerable to toxic encounters in new relationships. Yet even the initial interaction begins to provide feedback about the nourishing and toxic potentials of further contact.

In seeking new relationships, those who seem to continually encounter T people usually are out of touch with, or refuse to listen to, this feedback.

Toxic interaction is often described in terms of various "games"—since it requires at least two players, who must knowingly or unwittingly comply with the rules of the game. Usually these are not openly and clearly stated, yet each player follows an established pattern. Even in a long-standing relationship, when one person stops playing a particular game, the game is over.

In the case of Marilyn and Gregg, the initially nourishing relationship that Gregg hoped they could find never materialized. Rather than face this reality and confront himself with the painful fact that he loved Marilyn and didn't feel loved by her, he tried to live up to her expectations. In all good conscience, he hoped that if he did enough to please her, she would eventually respond and give him what he wanted. While he may have been victimized in the relationship, his attitude was also manipulative: *i.e.*, he played the "good boy" in the hope of getting his "payoff" in the form of a more loving and giving response from Marilyn.

HOW TO RECOGNIZE A POISONER: TWO SIDES OF THE SAME COIN

A person's self-poisoning behavior will inevitably be reflected in his way of relating to others. How a person poisons himself and how he relates to others in a poisonous manner are simply two sides of the same coin.

When Betty met Norman, he seemed to be just what she was looking for. All her life Betty wanted to be needed, and at twenty-seven she was beginning to feel that no man would ever really want her. Norman was clearly the neediest man she had ever met. "It was just a lucky chance that I caught him out in the open or he never would have met *anybody*!" she laughingly told one of her friends. Betty was referring to their initial meeting. Her landlord was away, and she had agreed to show a vacant apartment for him. Norman came to see it and rented it immediately. His shyness and fearfulness were obvious. Betty made repeated contact with Norman, and they gradually became friends. She consistently took the initiative in everything they did together. She often invited him to dinner and even cleaned his apartment, despite his mild protests.

Norman's fearfulness of people and fear of rejection were almost overwhelming. After two years of therapy, he still would not initiate contact. This was how he poisoned himself (refusing to reach out for what he needed). Betty gradually succeeded in becoming his security blanket. She readily took over any "problems" he encountered (*e.g.*, returning an appliance that was defective and that Norman would have given away rather than risk making the salesman angry).

Norman had found an ideal job for himself. After high school and two years in the Army Signal Corps, he went to work for the telephone company. After twelve years, he had become chief trouble shooter in charge of maintaining the automatic dialing equipment. He worked on a windowless floor of a large building filled with rows and rows of complex equipment. His contact with other employees was limited almost entirely to phone calls about equipment breakdowns. During these twelve years he had lived in the same apartment and had moved only because the building was to be torn down. His life style was one of rigid routine.

Betty brought excitement and interest into Norman's life. He was willing to explore new activities provided she was his companion (and guardian). It was only a question of time until Betty convinced Norman they should marry, and that took two years. A year later they had their first child, followed by a second and a third two years apart.

Norman had become increasingly dependent

on Betty, left all decisions to her. Now he also became exceedingly anxious about her and the children. Their oldest child was already unusually fearful. Despite his good intentions, Norman was poisoning his family with his apprehensiveness in the same way he poisoned himself. He was constantly phoning from work to make sure everything was all right. Betty's wish to be needed was fully gratified (and then some). Eventually, however, she became increasingly irritated by his obsessive fearfulness and felt more and more drained by his constant need to be reassured. She became even more annoyed when she realized that the children were also becoming excessively fearful and shy in response to Norman's way of relating to them.

Betty had sincerely intended to help Norman change for the better. Instead, as inevitably occurs, his way of relating to himself became his way of relating to those he loved. He could not give any more security to his family than he could give to himself. Since he had not found a solution for his own fearfulness, it was inevitable that he would instill this same fearfulness in those he loved.

A self-poisoner is usually fragmented, out of touch with or unresponsive to his essential needs. To expect him to be more capable of a nourishing relationship is wishful thinking. When a person's behavior is erratic and ineffective in responding to his own needs, how can he be expected to be more effective in his responsiveness to others?

HOW TO RECOGNIZE A POISONER:
NOURISHING AND TOXIC VIBRATIONS

T PERSON: Hello, I'm Mrs. M. and you looked so
interesting I decided I just had to meet you.
. . . This is my husband (*who nods and looks
away, half bored and half embarrassed*). . . . I
was here a whole week before I found out that
there was an internationally famous anthropolo-
gist staying here. . . . I was just dying to meet
him when I heard this. . . . I have so many
questions I've always wanted to know the answers to. . . . I learn a great deal from people
this way, without having to bother reading a
lot of books; and I know it makes him feel good
and important to give me the answers. What
do you do?

From the inception of a relationship there is a consistency about the other's behavior which sends dis-
tinct messages. Most people use a "scouting party"
technique automatically. However, they frequently
fail to listen to the messages they receive. The pain of
initial toxic encounters is often minimal and usually
causes only minor toxic reactions. Obviously, this is
due largely to the limited involvement. The N person is aware that the more of himself, his time, and
his energy he invests in the relationship, the more the
minor irritants may become major toxic experiences.
When he is anxious for a relationship or strongly
attracted to other qualities in another person, however, he frequently doesn't listen to disturbing messages. The more deprived he feels, the more intense
his need for involvement, the more he is apt to block

out the warnings (toxic vibrations) of a potentially toxic relationship. The willingness to look (with *all* the senses) and pay attention to how one is experiencing another is essential. How another person behaves even in trivial, momentary episodes will accurately reflect his over-all attitudes and way of relating to other people. When a person is interested in paying attention to the "vibrations" he receives from another, his own experience is the most reliable barometer of the other's nourishing and toxic potentials.

Each of us experiences some feedback when we meet someone new. Sometimes in our interest in establishing a new relationship, we admit negative feelings only in retrospect. ("I wanted to see him as being the kind of person I've been longing for.")

Despite their growing involvement and mutual interest in a sustained intimate relationship, Frank noticed how Ellen would look at other men and flirt with them. While this annoyed Frank, he decided that it was his own exaggerated jealousy and said nothing about it. They had agreed on an "open marriage," but the conditions had not been explicitly stated and accepted. Frank assumed their open marriage meant Ellen would continue her professional work as a beautician, as well as pursuing various independent interests and activities without him. Ellen wanted to continue having sexual relationships with other men. She had also decided that the best way to do this was secretly and discreetly. Frank had been very explicit in stating that extramarital affairs were totally unacceptable to him. When her flirtatiousness continued after they were married, he began to express his resentment and growing distrust. Ellen reassured him (while secretly deciding to be more subtle about her flirtations) and continued her affairs. Two years later, Frank discovered Ellen had been having affairs continuously before and since their marriage. Now it became obvious to him that all along there had been signs of Ellen's infidelity if only he had been willing to listen and pay attention to them. . . .

HOW TO RECOGNIZE A POISONER: THE TOXIC TOUCH

The atmosphere could scarcely have been warmer or more appealing. Rex had invited a dozen people for a weekend of skiing at his mountain lodge. Gina had accompanied her roommate, who had known Rex for some time. They were all sitting around the fire, joking and sharing the day's experiences. Gina was embarrassed by her reaction when Rex casually put his arm around her. It was a simple gesture of warmth which she noticed he made with everyone. Yet Gina found herself shivering. She was mystified by her reaction and did not understand herself at all. Later, they danced together and again she felt herself tense up for no apparent reason. Regardless of her lack of understanding, she told one of her friends later, "Something about him just turns me off." Gina declined when Rex tried to date her a week later.

Six months after the ski party, Rex married Sandra, Gina's former roommate. Four months after they were married, Sandra left Rex and got

an annulment. Only after their marriage had Sandra discovered that Rex insisted on what he called
an "old-fashioned–type marriage." He decided on
all their social activities, gave her a weekly list
of menus for each meal she was to prepare,
insisted that his wife select an entirely new wardrobe only in his presence, and refused to allow
her to purchase any clothing without his absolute
approval.

Sandra was far from the docile, compliant person she would have had to be to meet Rex's
demands. He absolutely refused to discuss these
issues, and in view of his insistent attitude despite
her protests, she left him. He tried to prevent her
from leaving by threats which made Sandra fear
for her physical safety.

Gina was aware that her palms were sweating
when she heard Sandra's story. Later, she
breathed a sigh of relief that she had paid attention to how she found herself responding to Rex
on the occasion of their first meeting.

Toxic people sometimes have "the touch of death."
There is something about their contact that elicits a
feeling of uneasiness. Other "toxic touchers" give one
the feeling of being squeezed, overwhelmed, or suffocated. Or, they make physical contact as if they did
not intend to let go. Infants become agitated and upset
when handled by toxic touchers and immediately quiet
down when someone else picks them up. (They
already have an intuitive ability to recognize a poisoner.)

When we pay attention to our reactions to being
touched, we learn to sense potentially poisonous peo-

ple. The warning signals ("Here comes a poisoner")
are not one-shot messages which a person must pick
up the first time around or miss his chance. There are
all kinds of corroborating messages that continue to
appear whenever toxic interaction is occurring.

HOW TO RECOGNIZE A POISONER: NOURISHING AND TOXIC VOICES

Lester was a thin, frail five-foot-three-inch man
who could tell a story in a most interesting manner. While everyone agreed that Lester had a
magnetic quality about him, somehow people
would begin to squirm and grow restless when he
made himself the center of attention. There was
a dignity about him that rendered people reluctant to interrupt him or even dare to make comments while he was talking. Typically, when he
began to tell a story, he would start with a dramatic flair; then his speech would slow down, and
he would utter a phrase, pause, and look around
to check that he still had everyone's attention. If
someone was looking away or seemed uninterested, he would pause even longer. People got
sucked into this game without even knowing what
was happening to them. It was as if they dared
not fail to pay attention or he would drag out his
story even longer. Gradually his voice would
become softer and lower until others had to lean
forward and strain to even hear his words. In this
way he would dominate a group. Within his cir-
cle of friends, he had set the mood of their
frequent dinner parties for several years. Sam, a
newcomer to the group, was an astute observer,

not one to gracefully accept being tortured: "God dammit, Lester, you're winding down again. Where's the key that will wind you up so that you can get your story over with or at least talk loud enough so that we can hear you without having to strain our ears?" With that single outburst of anger, Lester's friends were suddenly onto him.

It is often possible to recognize a poisoner by his voice alone. A nourishing person's voice sounds alive and exciting. His easy flow of words gives the listener a feeling of spontaneity. He sounds natural and real.

In contrast, the T person often speaks in a hypnotic monotone which drones on, boring other people or making it difficult for them to retain their interest in what he is saying. His voice may sound weak and scarcely audible. Or it may sound high-pitched or whining. Often his speech is a series of broken sentences. He begins, then stops, utters a few more words, and stops again. There is a lack of completeness in the statements, as if he were reluctant to be definite. When he is particularly threatened, his statements are filled with "maybes," "buts," and other qualifying phrases, as if to leave himself room to side-step any rejection or attack. Particularly when he is being personal he may stammer and stutter, even though this is not normally part of his speech pattern. His sentences ramble together, or his thoughts vacillate and change direction, so that it is difficult for the listener to follow what he is saying. While his toxic voice and way of speaking are usually not a premeditated way of tormenting his listeners, this does not lessen their poisonous effects on those who allow themselves to be victimized by politely playing "captive audience."

N people withdraw from or avoid such dialogues. In an ongoing relationship, an N person is open about how he is experiencing the other.

The N person expresses his annoyance as often as he needs to as a way of protecting himself from a toxic monologue or an irritating voice. He hopes (but doesn't expect or insist) that the other will hear him and respond by attempting to alleviate this disruption in their over-all relationship with each other. His attitude is not one of criticism but rather his statement (self-expression) of how he is experiencing the other. He is not "selling" anything, and if he finds that the other person is unwilling to acknowledge his requests, he takes responsibility for deciding what, if anything, he wishes to do about it.

HOW TO RECOGNIZE A POISONER: TOXIC VERBIAGE

While verbal communication is a powerful tool for reaching out to others for nourishment, verbiage can also be an intrusion. A person may feel charged with the energy of a "peak experience" and dissipate this energy prematurely with toxic verbiage. N people are selective and discriminating with their speech. Language itself is frequently an ineffective medium of communication. There are feelings and experiences that one human being can never fully communicate to another even with a most eloquent command of the language. Some experiences can never be conveyed to others in words. Nourishing people sense this and remain silent in order to nourish themselves to the fullest—particularly when an unusually enriching experience is occurring. The more meaningful a person's experience, even when it involves another, the less the likelihood that it is possible to share it verbally and the greater the likelihood that verbalizations will be toxic.

Toxic relationships are characterized by great masses of empty, meaningless verbiage as well as a sparsity of shared periods of silence or nonverbal communication.

In a nourishing relationship, each person is sensitive to when verbalizing would be toxic as well as when silence itself is a form of nourishment and sharing.

CHRONIC POISONING

Chronic poisoning includes both toxic interaction that is continually recurring between two people, and self-poisoning patterns that constantly recur in a person's ways of relating to himself. Chronic poisoning can be insidious, in that the frequent repetition of the pattern gradually dulls the person's awareness. He becomes habituated to the poison or takes it for granted as an unavoidable aspect of his life. His awareness may be manifested only in a slight sighing each time the process recurs. Like a person who for years has been thirty pounds overweight, the chronic poisoner is totally unaware of its drain on his energy.

For many years, Alfred appreciated his good fortune in having chosen interior design as his

profession. He enjoyed the challenge of each new
project and the many interesting people with
whom he came into contact. In most instances,
both he and his clients were well satisfied, and his
business had flourished.

Alfred would frequently ponder the sudden
tension he experienced as he drove home each
day. He loved his home and family, yet somehow
on arriving home, he needed his martini immediately. Usually his wife would have a drink ready
for him, and he would converse with her and the
children as long as they wished (provided this
did not interfere with his cocktails). He wondered
why he needed his drink so much. He decided
that it was just a habit that he had developed
over the years, and since he was not a heavy
drinker, it did not concern him. He would begin
to feel high with one drink and moderately inebri-
ated with the second . . . after which he felt
relaxed and sociable.

Then it happened. While vacationing in South
America, Alfred contracted a severe case of infectious hepatitis and he had to be hospitalized for
several weeks. After his recovery, his physician
instructed him to totally abstain from alcohol. He
continued to notice his chronic mood change when
he arrived home. Without his usual martinis, he
became increasingly tense as the evening wore on.
He was startled to discover how bored he was
with his wife's conversation. Most of her dialogue
was about trivial events of the day, her experiences with people he hardly knew, or requests
for money. In the past, Alfred (with the help of
his martinis) had politely listened to what was

now increasingly irritating, meaningless verbiage. His restlessness became more and more difficult to tolerate. He had always known that he was easily bored with trite conversations. However, he thought his love for his wife made him feel differently about her small talk.

Alfred's situation reached a crisis when he could no longer avoid confronting himself with the fact that he simply did not enjoy coming home. He became aware that in the past his boredom (mild, chronic poisoning) had been masked by his cocktail routine. He consulted a therapist, who suggested the whole family participate in the consultations (family therapy). The therapist encouraged them to converse with each other as they usually did at home. The trivial nature of their conversation soon became apparent to everyone. Other members of the family admitted that they too were usually bored. The children in particular expressed their resentment about the small talk their parents made and confessed that often they quietly snickered to each other about "how silly Mom and Dad are," making such a big thing about minor incidents and decisions.

With their new-found awareness, they began to experiment with ways of alleviating the chronic boredom which, as it turned out, plagued not only Alfred but the rest of the family as well. Alfred also began to explore more stimulating ways to spend his evenings, including more unshared activities that he found enjoyable and relaxing.

ESTABLISHING NOURISHING RELATIONSHIPS

It takes two people to sustain a toxic relationship. When one person's attitudes and behavior are nourishing and nonmanipulative, a toxic relationship does not continue.

Nourishing attitudes are the foundation for a nourishing relationship as well as for effective antidotes to existing toxic relationships.

As soon as we meet someone, we begin initiating various kinds of contact. "Contact" means sharing part of oneself with another. Mutual contacting and feedback (expressing how we experience another's expression) are the beginning of a relationship. As this contacting continues, we discover more about each other and become increasingly aware of our reactions and feelings toward each other. When this is primarily a mutually nourishing experience, the relationship is most likely to continue and deepen. We begin to lower our defensive barriers as initial feelings of threat or apprehension diminish.

In a nourishing relationship each person's identity remains clear and separate.

As we open more of ourselves, our vulnerability increases. This is an inevitable part of an intimate relationship. We also become increasingly dependent on the other for the satisfaction of various emotional needs. It is in this sense that the expression "being emotionally involved" is meaningful.

In such a relationship, mutual respect for each other's feelings of inadequacy and sensitive areas is particularly important. Without care and respect, two people can hurt each other deeply when they are angry, since each knows where the other's raw nerve endings lie. In a nourishing relationship, this kind of poisonous interaction is avoided.

In intimate contacting and sharing, much of what is expressed is not meaningful to the other. A man may not care about his wife's club activities and listens because *she* wants to tell him about it, but finds himself neither stimulated nor interested in pursuing the subject further. A woman may not particularly care how many refrigerators her husband sold and may listen out of consideration for *his* need to share this portion of himself. It is a legitimate part of their relationship in that it has meaning for one of them. They listen because they care about the other and what the other needs—someone to listen.

To sustain a nourishing relationship, we must be aware above all of our own unique self and understand that the relationship, however intimate, is subordinate to this self.

Giving up our personal identity does not lead to intimacy. Each of us has needs that we must fulfill outside a single relationship, no matter how intimate it may be. Each of us needs contact with other people. Each of us has interests that must be pursued separately. Each needs solitude and activities that involve only himself. In a nourishing relationship, these unshared areas are accepted (recognized as part of the reality of each self).

There are also "no man's lands" within us all. These are unshared areas of the self about which we are extremely sensitive, and we will react in a hostile, belligerent manner when they are intruded upon. In a nourishing relationship, it is understood that such areas are "off limits." In a marriage, for instance, one person may resent any criticism of his family. Each spouse must learn to avoid these areas. The failure to recognize and accept these limitations sets the stage for poisonous relating.

Toxic patterns also develop when one person persists in seeking some kind of interaction which the other person resents and rejects. This happens when one person decides to "change" some aspect of the other's behavior against his wishes.

HE: *(After having intercourse)* Did you come?

SHE: *(Rather embarrassed)* I don't like to talk about that.

HE: I'm not just curious. I want to feel that I satisfied you.

SHE: I may be old-fashioned, but I get uncomfortable talking about these things.

HE: I know how you feel. I used to get embarrassed about that myself. If you try talking about it, you'll find that gradually you'll get used to it.

SHE: That may be so, but I really don't want to. I don't like talking about how I experience sex.

HE: How am I going to know whether I satisfy you or not?

SHE: I'll tell you what I feel I want to tell you. I wish you wouldn't push me on this.

HE: Well, just tell me this one time. Did you come or not?

SHE: This kind of conversation really turns me off— and I mean that in the sexual way, too. I don't want to feel I have to report to you whether I came or not when we have intercourse.

HE: I don't want to be persistent about it; I just like to ask you about it occasionally.

SHE: I'm really beginning to get angry with you. I wish you'd stop bugging me.

A nourishing attitude by her lover would be exemplified by the following statement either to himself or to her: "I accept (recognize how strongly you feel about) your unwillingness to discuss your orgasm. I would prefer that you were willing to be more open about this. But it is more important for me to avoid turning you off sexually, so I'll stop bothering you about it."

Developing an intimate relationship includes discovering a person's "no man's lands" and doing our best to avoid them.

In a nourishing relationship, each person communicates what attitudes, behavior, or sharing are unacceptable to him. Essentially, these represent areas of the two selves that are incompatible and irreconcilable. Presumably they will never blend into a harmonious aspect of their nourishing relationship (nor is this necessary).

A nourishing, intimate relationship is limited to those experiences that both either want or are willing to share with each other.

NOURISHING AND TOXIC CONFLICT

Conflict in a relationship means the existence of opposing needs between two people which is expressed in a struggle against each other. Either (or both) experiences the other as an opposing force standing between him and what he needs. In the face of opposition, N people fight for what they need and protect themselves against infringements from others. In intimate relationships, they see conflict as a constructive attempt to resolve issues between themselves and the other. In nourishing conflict, some resolution or compromise is reached. The issue is somehow settled, or the situation creating the conflict is modified in a mutually acceptable manner.

In contrast, a toxic conflict is characterized by chronic aggressiveness and a struggle that remains unresolved and unfinished. The energy of each person is continually dissipated in a battle of attack and counterattack in which each uses his particular arsenal of weapons (games and manipulations). In an ongoing relationship, the "unfinished business" of toxic conflicts appears in the form of periodic eruptions of new battles over the same old war. Toxic conflict is characteristically filled with transitory experiences of "victory" and "defeat."

In a nourishing conflict, the person is more aware of how he experiences the struggle, the amount of energy he is using, and whether the issue is worth his effort. N people rarely feel the necessity of fighting an all-out, do-or-die battle. Their purpose is more specific, and their capacity to find an acceptable solution is greater.

The N person avoids endless conflict. When he feels the conflict is not resolvable or is gradually merging into a vague struggle, he is more apt to disengage. He accepts the reality that many conflicts in a relationship are not resolved and that this does not necessarily jeopardize the relationship.

While N people are more sensitive to when their conflicts are jeopardizing their entire relationship, T people tend to ignore the consequences in their persistent endeavor to prove their point. Frequently, their aggressiveness is an ego trip in which their battling is not determined by the importance to them of the issue in question. Rather, they battle for toxic reasons: to maintain their image or to compensate for their insecurity and lack of self-esteem. The toxic person frequently gets bogged down in a chronically aggressive pattern with others and ignores (refuses to consider) the time and energy he uses up in his struggle.

In a nourishing conflict, a creative solution often evolves from the struggle. When the conflict is resolved in this way, the resolution brings with it the excitement and enthusiasm of emerging possibilities of adding something new, different, or creative to the relationship. The conflict has been "finished," and the air has been cleared.

Only rarely in a nourishing relationship is an issue so vital that each person feels an essential aspect of his integrity is at stake *and* that the only solution to the conflict is for one person to give in to the other. It is relatively infrequent that an honest, legitimate conflict of interest exists in such a vital area of each self. When this is the case, a critical, "irreconcilable difference" may exist, and it is more likely that the relationship will terminate.

Toxic conflict also occurs when the struggle becomes primarily an occasion for each person to dump his frustrations on the other, rather than for settling issues. This encourages a chronic stalemate in which the real areas of disagreement become buried under an avalanche of trivia. The intensity and extent of the struggle become increasingly inappropriate to the particular incident involved.

We must be aware of the process that occurs between people in conflict if we are to distinguish whether a particular argument is nourishing or toxic. When a person is clearly aware of what he wants to accomplish, he is able to see the significance of the struggle within the context of the relationship as a whole. In intimate relationships, the more ongoing the conflict that occurs, and the wider the range of issues about which the two people feel they need to oppose each other, the greater the likelihood that the conflict is toxic.

The antidote to toxic conflict is most clearly suggested in the way N people fight. They struggle *for* what they want as an expression of their self, their needs, and their identity. They also avoid fighting *against* the other person in an effort to subdue him or move him out of his position.

While it is true that manipulation is toxic to an intimate relationship, it is also true that everyone manipulates at times. The antagonistic difference in the nature of manipulative and intimate behavior is essentially irreconcilable.

Intimacy is the hallmark of a nourishing relationship, and manipulation is the hallmark of toxic relating.

Nourishing manipulation can be described as more open, honest, and direct. The person shares his intent with the person whom he wants to manipulate. He also asks the other to allow himself to go along with the manipulation.

Toxic manipulation by a mother toward her bed-wetting seven-year-old is illustrated in the following example:

"Jimmy, I'm going to get you to stop wetting your bed if I have to wake you every hour to do it. I'm really ashamed that you still wet your bed at your age. What will people think? In fact, if you don't stop wetting your bed, I'm going to tell your friends about it. How do you like *that*?"

Nourishing manipulation:

> "Jimmy, there's a device I can buy for your bed that rings a buzzer to wake you up when you start wetting. Would you be willing to try it? Do you have any other suggestions how I might help you? Also, I would like you to change your sheets whenever you do wet the bed and put the wet ones in the washing machine."

NOURISHING AND TOXIC COMPROMISE

When we are interested in more than a transient relationship, we cannot always "do our own thing." Relating in this way is comparable to the supertoxic attitude of the person who insists on acting out every impulse. There is a difference between being aware of what we want and satisfying these needs without regard for the context or the consequence of one's action. To insist on always having our way—or being resentful when we can't—is essentially to ignore the existence of other people. This reflects an indifference to mutual nourishment and an insistence on a "one-way-street" relationship. ("I'm willing to continue our relationship only as long as I have my way!") No two people harmonize to such a degree that their needs are always mutually blending.

In a nourishing relationship, compromise is a foregone conclusion.

In nourishing compromise, each person is aware that his flow of needs is different from the other's and that it is not possible at the moment to respond to his own need and the other person's as well. Nourishing compromise is a willingness to give another at least part of what he wants and to relegate some of one's own needs to a secondary position, at least temporarily. In addition, a nourishing compromise lacks any hidden expectations that the other will reciprocate later on. In a nourishing compromise, when there is some contract or agreement ("I'll pick the movie tonight; you pick the movie the next time"), the expectation is explicitly stated and agreed upon. The compromising is done freely and willingly. Cajoling, threatening, or pressuring the other into compromising at best creates only superficial harmony, while an undercurrent of toxic interaction is likely to begin.

Any pressure (intrusion), even in a loving relationship, creates feelings of resentment. These do not necessarily affect the relationship significantly. Irritation, annoyance, and other resentments are inevitable. However, they are increasingly apt to become toxic when one person's pattern of relating has a continually annoying effect on the other.

HUSBAND: Hurry up, honey—we'll be late for dinner at Mother's.

WIFE: I'm doing the best I can. The children are still dressing.

HUSBAND: Well, hurry them up.

WIFE: They are hurrying. Janet just got home from her piano lesson.

H.: Can't she have her lesson earlier?

W: (*Getting annoyed*) She's in school earlier—remember? Your daughter *does* go to school, you know!

H: Mother gets upset when we're late.

W: Your nagging every time we go to your mother's spoils the whole evening for me. If she won't set the time later, she'll just have to wait.

H: Okay, I agree. Let me know if there is anything I can do to help the kids get ready.

In this example, the husband becomes aware that he is relating to his wife in a toxic manner. He is pushing her on the basis of his own anxiety and ignoring the effect on her of *his* need to hurry. Toward the end of the dialogue, he becomes aware of her feelings and his attitude is less toxic and more nourishing.

In a nourishing relationship both people accept the reality that there will be disagreements that cannot be solved by compromise. Each person then takes responsibility for his own unfulfilled needs and does the best he can to satisfy them without attempting to coerce the other.

Toxic compromising is based on maneuvers, manipulations, and pressures that one or both persons employ against the other. Disagreements are settled on some kind of psychic battlefield. When this is an ongoing pattern in the relationship, endless war exists in which each fights the other to get what he wants. It matters little who "wins" or "loses," since the end result is the gradual destruction of the relationship.

HUSBAND: Why in the hell aren't you and the kids ready? Do you always have to express your resentment toward my mother by being late every time she invites us to dinner?

WIFE: It would be easier if your mother didn't insist on inviting us on a school night.

HUSBAND: Oh! She should arrange her life to suit you!

WIFE: You just don't give a damn how much I have to rush getting myself and the children ready while you read your newspaper.

H: You want me to do *your* work after I've been chasing customers all day? I'm supposed to be your maid also?

W: *(Bitterly sarcastic)* Thanks a lot. You're such a loving husband. *You* can go alone or take the kids as they are. *I'm* not going at all!

H: Oh, no! You're going or else you can just forget about ever having *your* parents over here again.

NOURISHING AND TOXIC TRUST

T people feel guilty when they distrust another person. A self-poisoner may even feel this way with someone he has just met or with whom he has only a superficial relationship. He may feel sheepish about asking a salesman to write on the sales contract all the specifications promised with his purchase. When he feels distrustful in an intimate relationship, guilt over this feeling is apt to be greatly intensified. Children, for example, sense when others are not being honest, yet are frequently unwilling to openly acknowledge their distrust. They have been taught that it's "not nice." In adult relationships, T people often become anxious about feeling suspicious. Similarly, when confronted with the question "Don't you trust me?" their usual reaction is embarrassment, discomfort, and anxiety, as if distrust were evil or shameful.

Distrust is a feeling that we often cannot adequately verbalize even to ourselves. Refusing to admit distrust sets the stage for a phony game-playing relationship. If a person is unwilling to allow himself the freedom to be openly distrustful, he either manipulates himself or begins manipulative games with the other, or both.

The more often a person has been deceived, the more suspicious he will become. Such an attitude can become exceedingly toxic. Living in the now does not mean throwing away one's past experiences—but it does mean evaluating the present on its own terms. Being either too trusting or too naïve is toxic to one-self.

BEING IN TOUCH

An individual's responsiveness to the needs of another is not constant. Rather, a person's ability and willingness to give nourishment in an ongoing relationship vary widely over a period of time. Being in touch with the other person consists of being sensitive to and aware of his availability as a source of nourishment at any particular moment. Toxic interaction often begins with a lack of awareness of where the other person is: *i.e.*, how approachable and available he is at the moment. Without some awareness of the mood of the other before contact is initiated, a person risks the angry rejection of one who feels intruded upon simply because he was "in a bad place" beforehand.

Raymond P. went to work at six in the morning and returned at eight or nine o'clock each evening, in a state of semiexhaustion. His wife complained that they had little or no relationship: "He comes home exhausted, and when he takes a day off, he stays in bed or watches TV. I've told him we're drifting apart, but he just shrugs it off."

Although her complaint seems reasonable, it becomes irrelevant (poisonous) when she *continually* finds her husband unresponsive. She is apt to frustrate herself less if she is willing to accept (recognize) the reality of their relationship. A nourishing attitude when he is consistently unwilling to respond to her would center on taking responsibility for herself to satisfy her needs in other ways. It is an open question whether she will be able to adequately relieve her frustrations in some other way. Her best efforts in this attempt may not be adequate, yet this remains the best she can do.

It is futile to blame Mr. P. for the deteriorating relationship between himself and his wife. Any marriage is a two-way street. The best the wife can do is try to share her feelings with her husband. She does this primarily to express herself rather than to make demands which only lead to toxic manipulations. She is aware that it is up to him if he chooses to be more responsive to her.

No rule or formula can replace human sensitivity and responsiveness. The more frequently one asks for something from another and the more consistently the requests are rejected, the greater the likelihood that the intimacy of the relationship will deteriorate.

Human communication is grossly imprecise and subject to constant error in interpretation. In addition, people do not consistently send the same message, nor are they uniformly accepting or rejecting of the same request or offer. Knowing when to persist and when to back off is the key to an emotionally nourishing relationship.

Much poisonous interaction occurs when one person refuses to tune in to the other. Being exclusively on one's "own trip" invariably leads to toxic relationships, since this attitude ignores the integrity of the other person. N people are more aware of the ongoing responsiveness and reactions of the other. Their sensitivity makes their requests more appealing, since it reflects a greater awareness of the other person's needs and wants.

> Mrs. R. finally left her husband. Only then did he take her requests seriously (give up his one-way-street relating). He agreed to marital counseling, in which he admitted for the first time that his wife was nagging him to work less for his own good. He was utterly bewildered (reflecting how out of touch he still was) when she reacted to his explanation with even greater despair and hopelessness. Shortly thereafter, she divorced him.

Even in the most intimate and loving relationships, too much toxic interaction can bring the relationship to the point at which one or both partners lose all desire to continue the relationship.

TAKING A STAND

While toxic processes are continuously present in our environment, poisonous interaction can become so intense that sometimes we decide we have had it and must "take a stand." In such instances, the N person is able to mobilize his resources and provide himself with "psychic space." He uses his power to counter the poisoning process. The N person is by no means always mild-mannered and diplomatic. He is capable of taking his stand with great determination. The antidotes to toxic intrusions sometimes demand tremendous counterforce. The N person kills a rattlesnake when he discovers it in his own back yard; he does not chase it back into the bushes because he is a humane person. Sometimes his behavior may be extremely aggressive, but it is rarely cruel or sadistic. The N person is simply determined to do the best he can to sustain his own health and protect himself from being poisoned.

Taking a stand means defining oneself to others. When a person always says yes to the other, he gives the impression that he is an endless giver, a tireless nourisher. It is impossible for us to convey who we are without saying no. Taking a stand involves innumerable limitations which can be communicated by no's, refusals, and active rejecting.

The T person often resists saying no and is willing to poison himself rather than take a clear stand and set limits on what he is willing to give. Often his no's come only as a last resort, when his reserves are depleted and he feels his back is against the wall. He is then apt to violently explode. Others who are unaware of his accumulative self-poisoning pattern are often bewildered by the sudden, explosive nature of his rejection, which may be precipitated by some trivial incident.

THE NEED TO ANNIHILATE

Sometimes so much toxic behavior has occurred and the poisonous processes have become so intense that the person involved resolves to terminate the relationship. He may feel totally uninterested in the other, not wanting to ask anything or give anything. Or he may become irritable or angry at the slightest conflict or the mere presence of the other. Often the person feels his integrity has been so violated that any further relationship is intolerable. He may be so filled with rage that the process may even feel pleasurable.

There is a phase in relationships in which antidotes are no longer possible; the relationship has become so toxic that it has reached a point of no return. The longer this feeling persists, the greater the likelihood that terminating the relationship is the only realistic solution. The need to annihilate the other is the most extreme consequence of toxic relating. It is in essence the death (by poison) of the relationship.

NOURISHING AND TOXIC RESPONSIBILITY

While the nourishing person feels a responsibility toward other people and a concern for their well-being, he does not automatically respond to their needs. His responsiveness is regulated by his wanting to give and his *willingness* to respond to others.

Mrs. Larson was a wealthy widow who made large annual donations to various philanthropic causes. For years she had insisted that she be solicited only by mail and that her donations remain anonymous.

Toxic responsibility is filled with shoulds, external injunctions, and feelings of obligation and guilt. It is usually experienced as a chore, in which the only gratification is getting it finished. The responsiveness of T people to others is largely based on fear of punishment, disapproval, or loss of face if they don't comply with what is expected of them. Or, they respond as a way of manipulating others ("Now you owe me").

Taking responsibility for ourselves means responding to our own needs (response-ability). This includes being responsible for the appropriateness of our behavior within the context (environment) in which we are thinking, feeling, and acting. Whenever we initiate an action, it usually elicits a counter-action. While we cannot control the world, we are responsible to some degree for the counter-action we instigate. If, for example, a person decides to ventilate his pent-up frustrations toward a friend who has annoyed him by some trivial act, he takes upon himself the risk of destroying the friendship.

On the other hand, we are not responsible for the basic happiness and unhappiness of those closest to us. It is toxic to expect someone else to take charge of one's life.

Mr. S. followed his wife around like a loyal puppy dog: "I just love being with you, and I want to share everything with you." He would go with her to the market in the evenings and shop-

ping with her on weekends. He would spend
hours with her while she shopped for her clothing. Mrs. S. enjoyed much of their sharing of
activities and interests.

Mr. S. was perplexed when his wife became
increasingly irritable at their "togetherness." When
she decided to enroll alone in an adult education
course, a crisis ensued. Her husband insisted that
she was abandoning him.

Mr. S. was phobic about being alone. He "used"
his wife as a way of avoiding his fear and anxiety
about being on his own. He insisted that if she
loved him, she would not cause him such pain by
going away one evening every week. In essence,
he wanted her to take responsibility for resolving
his anxiety, his fear, and his pain.

He was perplexed by her new-found attitude:
"I love you. I want you to be happy, *and* I am
not responsible for making you happy. I will share
what I want to share—not what you expect me
to share." He refused to hear (accept) what his
wife was trying to communicate and insisted on
his feelings of being cruelly abandoned: "How
can you leave me for something you don't have to
do when you know that I'm sitting here at home
suffering and unhappy while you're enjoying yourself?"

This is the kind of manipulative responsibility that
destroys relationships. It is an example of toxic use of
love and intimacy.

> In a nourishing relationship, regardless of the depth of the love and caring, one person is not responsible (obligated) to do something about the pain, frustration, and anxiety of the other.

Rather, it is the person's choice how much he wishes to respond to the other and in what ways. It is also his choice (and responsibility to himself) to set limits on his givingness. An example of a nourishing response (antidote) from Mrs. S. would be as follows:

"I am concerned and feel badly about your anxiety when I leave you alone. I feel that I share a great deal with you, and I enjoy being with you. However, I also need some activities away from you, even though I love you deeply."

It is an honest reaction if Mr. S. continues to resent his wife's attitude; he doesn't have to like it. However, if he is interested in sustaining their nourishing relationship, he is willing to accept (recognize the existence of) her need regardless of his own feelings. In contrast, a toxic response would be to continue to make her feel guilty, or to otherwise manipulate her in the hope that she will give up her independent activities.

Mr. S.: "Well, it's Wednesday, so I guess you're going to leave me again. Aren't you finished punishing me yet? Haven't you proved your point that you can be independent?"

This is the kind of "bear-trap question" that is most apt to precipitate still more poisonous interaction by continuing to magnify the issue into a major conflict.

The antidote to many such toxic interactions in intimate relationships is the willingness to take responsibility for one's self rather than expect the other to do this.

There is a difference between intimacy and stickiness. Often the way two people relate is filled with some poisonous qualities of which neither of them might be aware. Cultural myths have frequently ingrained fantastic expectations of what an intimate relationship is or should be. For example:

If you loved me, you'd want to share the things I love to do.

If you loved me, you wouldn't object to my wanting to do what I need to do for myself: have an extramarital affair.

If you loved me, you wouldn't refuse—especially without a good reason—when I ask you for something.

If you loved me, you wouldn't hurt me by getting angry at me when I do something you don't like.

In an intimate relationship, the individuality and integrity of each person is accepted as basic. Their separate selves remain the center of each person's existence. This is not only acknowledged by the other, but appreciated as well. "Stickiness" is a contrasting way of relating in which one or both persons seek to merge their identities (confluence) and lose their separate selves. Confluence, except for brief periods such as during sexual intercourse, is toxic to sustained intimate relating. It corrodes the autonomous, self-initiating qualities of each person which constitute the basic reservoir of their ability to continue to contribute more of their selves (giving and nourishing) to each other.

CHANGING INDEBTEDNESS TO APPRECIATION

When a person feels a debt of gratitude toward another, he feels under pressure to respond in order to get off the hook. Being given to is then not a joy but an obligation.

The person who feels indebted is easily victimized by people who play "You owe me" games. Toxic parents often remind their children that "without me you would not be in this world": the child "owes" them his existence. Even in adulthood he may continue to feel burdened by this debt and guilt-ridden when he doesn't pay off by remaining "dutiful." He may continue to submit to this chronic poisoning indefinitely, or he can thank (appreciate) them for what they have given him and declare the "debt" null and void.

In contrast, N people appreciate other people and what they have given. "Appreciation" has the flavor of a finished situation, in which the recipient does not feel an obligation to respond as if to balance a ledger. The appreciative person has the relaxed attitude of one who has enjoyed something pleasurable which is now finished. He doesn't feel any strings attached to his present or future relationship with the other person. While he may feel available or even eager to give to the other, he feels free to give when and how he wants to, rather than because of an old obligation.

NOURISHING AND TOXIC GIVING

A giving person can poison himself with his giving. Toxic givers are easy pickings for those who survive by endlessly sucking nourishment from others while giving little in return. Frequently they play "Red Cross Lady" by continually giving solely on the basis of what the other person wants. While the enjoyment of giving and pleasing others can be very nourishing, it becomes self-poisoning when the person ignores the limits of his ability to give and stops only when he is exhausted. The self-poisoning giver often seems plagued by a compulsive altruism in which he chooses to neglect his own needs rather than say no to others.

The nourishing giver does not give in a random, indiscriminate manner. He chooses when, how often, and to whom he wants to give and does not feel uncomfortable if he decides to stop. Still more important, he does not feel he deserves repayment.

The toxic giver always expects some response from the other. His giving is a form of manipulation in which he is looking for a pay-off. Toxic giving is *primarily* motivated by some need other than the spontaneous desire or willingness to give. The person who gives out of guilt, for example, is "paid off" by a feeling of good conscience, of having done his duty. His giving lacks the quality of a positive expression of his self. Instead, he experiences *primarily* a sense of relief. Similarly, giving out of fear reflects an apprehensiveness about subsequent rejection. Giving out of shame or embarrassment is motivated primarily by the need to look good in the eyes of one's fellow men.

A person's refusal to allow others to give to him is also toxic. There are people who won't let anyone do anything for them and reject the givingness of others politely but with an emphatic attitude. At first they may appear merely to play the game of wanting to be coaxed, but it soon becomes apparent that they mean business. They may refuse gifts, favors, and social invitations whenever possible. They would rather be the host continually than accept the hospitality of others or the need of others to reciprocate.

Excessive self-nourishing becomes toxic when the person rejects his legitimate needs for gratification and nourishment from others (the need to be given to). He is, after all, a social animal. He would rather have someone else scratch his back than scratch it himself—even if he could reach it.

CONCLUSION

All toxic patterns are basically self-induced and are secondarily reflected in one's relationships with others. It is each person's responsibility when he allows others to poison him or initiates poisonous interaction himself.

For each person interested in the antidotes to toxic behavior, the ongoing question always remains "What can *I* do to avoid being poisoned, *and* what can I do to minimize being poisonous to myself or others?"

Mistakes are not only an inevitable part of any learning process: they are also an essential ingredient in this process. Without the experience of frustration from errors, misjudgments, miscalculations, and other "mistakes," there would be no tension (frustrated needs) to effectively motivate a person to experiment with new, more gratifying ways of being and relating. The critical issue is whether or not the person learns from his mistakes. When a person is unaware, his mistakes are futile, frustrating experiences that endlessly drain his energies.

Toxic experiences are a necessary part of discovering antidotes. A person cannot prepare for living ahead of time. One learns about toxic interaction only by experiencing toxic relating. The question is whether the person is aware of his toxic experiences and whether he learns how to protect himself more effectively against them.

Any time a person is pushed, he will push back. The intricacies of this process are endless. A parent dominates (pushes) his child and is astonished that in adolescence the child becomes unmanageable (finally has the power to push back). A man "proves" to his wife by quoting from sexologists that any kind of sexual foreplay is "normal," so why won't she agree? He then can't understand her growing frigidity and avoidance of his advances (the counterpush).

The antidote to toxic interaction in a relationship is best discovered by mutual awareness and an attitude of respect for each other's integrity.

The more willing each person is to give nourishment to others and to minimize his own toxic relating, the more likely he is to experience nourishment in return and the greater will be his resistance to the toxicities of others. When a person relates honestly and authentically, he has done all he can to encourage the other to relate to him in the same way. In so doing, he guarantees himself nothing. This too he accepts, by letting go of his expectations. On a gut level, he believes that, in intimate relating, nobody owes anybody anything.